CULTURE SMART!

UGANDA

Ian Clarke

·K·U·P·E·R·A·R·D·

ISBN 978 1 85733 699 3
This book is also available as an e-book: eISBN 978 1 85733 700 6

British Library Cataloguing in Publication Data
A CIP catalogue entry for this book is available from the British Library

First published in Great Britain
by Kuperard, an imprint of Bravo Ltd
59 Hutton Grove, London N12 8DS
Tel: +44 (0) 20 8446 2440   Fax: +44 (0) 20 8446 2441
www.culturesmart.co.uk
Inquiries: sales@kuperard.co.uk

Distributed in the United States and Canada
by Random House Distribution Services
1745 Broadway, New York, NY 10019
Tel: +1 (212) 572-2844   Fax: +1 (212) 572-4961
Inquiries: csorders@randomhouse.com

Series Editor Geoffrey Chesler
Design Bobby Birchall

Printed in Malaysia

About the Author

IAN CLARKE has lived in Uganda for more than twenty-five years. Born in Northern Ireland, where he trained as a doctor, he is a naturalized Ugandan citizen, and as the Mayor of Makindye Division of Kampala is the only elected white politician in the country. He first came to Uganda after the civil war ended in 1986, and since then has witnessed the country's development. He writes a weekly social commentary in the *Sunday Vision*, Uganda's leading national newspaper, and is the author of two books about his experience of Uganda, *The Man with the Key has Gone*, and *How Deep is This Pothole?* He has founded two hospitals: Kiwoko Mission Hospital and International Hospital Kampala. He is also the founder of the International Health Science University in Kampala. Dr. Clarke lives in Uganda with his wife and family.

contents

contents

Map of Uganda

introduction

Once notorious for the tyranny of Idi Amin, immortalized in the film *The Last King of Scotland*, Uganda has for the last twenty-eight years struggled to overcome its negative image. In this it has largely been successful, though not without some glitches along the way.

Uganda was rated "best tourist destination" of 2013 by *National Geographic* magazine. In addition to its game parks, home to the Big Five, it has the largest number of recorded bird species of any country, making it the richest African destination for birders. It is also the home of the famed mountain gorillas, and the mighty River Nile provides some of the best whitewater rafting in the world. Add to this an almost perfect climate and spectacular sightseeing, including the source of the Nile, Murchison Falls, the "little Switzerland" of Kabale, the volcanic lakes, and the Rwenzori Mountains, and one can understand why Winston Churchill called Uganda "the Pearl of Africa."

But Uganda not only has wildlife and natural beauty to offer; the Ugandan people are what make it different. Drawn from over twenty tribes, they represent a rich blend of traditions and culture. You can sample this in dance and song performances by groups such as the Ndere Troupe in Kampala, or you can wander through a village, and get to know the local people, since English is widely spoken. You will find them sociable, warm, and hospitable. Kampala is famous as the social capital of East Africa, the city that never sleeps, where every kind of nightlife is on offer, and Ugandans have now been officially rated the happiest people in East Africa by the UN *World Happiness Report 2013*! It was noted in the report that it was not the high quality of life that made them happier than their neighbors, but their positive, optimistic outlook on life. Perhaps the years of adversity have made them appreciate the little that they have. This national characteristic, where Ugandans have traditionally shared what they have, makes them special. It is not possible to call in at a mealtime and leave without partaking of the family meal, and probably also being given a live chicken to take home.

The Uganda of today is a unique blend of beauty, tradition, and modernity. The media is free and there are always lively debates on current political, social, or religious issues, where your opinion is welcomed. Despite this, the visitor will generally need to reach out to Ugandans first as they have seen many foreigners come and go, who are not really interested in their lives, and if you don't bother with them they will not bother with you. However, once you demonstrate your interest, they will accept you with open arms.

Inevitably there are cultural pitfalls for the unwary traveler—differences in expectations, customs, and ways of behaving. This book provides key insights into Ugandan life and offers practical tips on how best to meet the Ugandan people on their own terms—vital information for tourists and businesspeople alike.

Key Facts

Official Name	Republic of Uganda	
Capital City	Kampala	
Main Cities and Towns	Jinja, Entebbe, Masaka, Mbarara, Fort Portal, Kabale, Gulu, Lira, Kisoro, Mbale, Arua, Kasesse, Iganga, Tororo, Busia, Kotido	
Area	93,065.29 sq. miles (241,038 sq. km)	Slightly smaller than Oregon
Geography	Bordered by Kenya, South Sudan, the Democratic Republic of the Congo, Rwanda, Tanzania, and Lakes Edward, Albert, and Victoria.	Lowest point: Lake Albert 2,037 ft (621 m). Highest point: Margherita Peak on Mount Stanley 16,765.09 ft (5,110 m)
Regions	4 regions: Central, Northern, Eastern and Western; 111 districts	
Terrain	Mostly plateau with a rim of mountains. Three main types of terrain: swamps, fertile plateau with wooded hills, and semi-arid areas in the northwest. Uganda has 60 protected areas, including 10 national parks.	
Climate	Tropical with two dry seasons (December to February, June to August)	Uganda is more temperate than the surrounding areas due to its altitude.
Population	33,640,833 (growth rate 3.3%)	
Age Structure	0–14 years: 48.9% ; 15–24 years: 21.2% ; 25–54 years: 25.5%; 55–64 years: 2.3% ; 65 years and over: 2.1% (2013 est.)	

Uganda GDP	US $19.80 billion in 2012	GDP per capita is US $405.
Natural Resources	Copper, cobalt, hydropower, limestone, salt, arable land, the Nile, gold, petroleum	
Currency	Uganda Shilling (UGX)	1 USD = 2,622.00 UGX (2014 rate)
Language	English is the official language, with Swahili as the second national language.	Luganda is the most widely spoken tribal language in Central District. Other tribal languages spoken in the northern, western and eastern regions.
Religion	Predominantly Christian, with 42% Protestant, 42% Catholic. Muslim 13%, others 3%.	
Government	Multiparty Democratic Republic	
Media	Relative press freedom. Newspapers: *New Vision, Daily Monitor, Observer, Independent, Red Pepper*	TV stations: NTV, UBC, NBS, WBS, Bukedde. Many local radio stations. Social media widely accessed
Electricity	240 volts, 50 Hz	British 3-prong rectangular blade plugs
TV/Video	PAL B/G system	Digital and analogue
Internet Domain	.ug	
Telephone	Country code 256	Main city codes: Entebbe 42, Jinja 43, Kampala 41, Kyambogo 41
Time Zone	GMT + 3 hours	

chapter one

LAND & PEOPLE

GEOGRAPHY

Uganda straddles the Equator. It lies within the Nile basin on the East African plateau, at an average of 3,609 feet (1,100 meters) above sea level, and shares borders with South Sudan to the north, Kenya to the east, the Democratic Republic of Congo (DRC) to the west, Rwanda to the southwest, and Tanzania to the south, with which it shares a large part of Lake Victoria. Other major lakes include Lake Kyoga in the center and Lakes Albert, George, and Edward on the Congolese border. Although not an enormous country, like Sudan or Tanzania, Uganda is still the size of the

British Isles, and many of the game parks, or areas of outstanding beauty, are six to eight hours' drive from the capital, Kampala. Murchison Falls, to the north, where all the waters of the Nile cascade through a twenty-six-foot (8-meter) wide gorge, is a spectacular sight, as are the fat crocodiles that bask in the sun near the foot of the falls. These prehistoric creatures have found the most favorable of habitats, where they feast on the fish that are stunned by their journey through the rushing waters of the Falls.

Murchison Falls National Park itself has a grand wilderness feel, where one instinctively senses that nature has not yet been tamed and wildlife reigns. The elephants are bigger than in many other parts of Africa, the buffalo herds larger, and the giraffes more majestic. Kidepo Game Reserve in Karamoja, in the northeast, is even wilder, perhaps because of its remoteness. Climbing the Rwenzori Mountains can be arduous, involving a trek through steep terrain, swamps, and glaciers for six days, but those who have completed it come back with tales of

incredible natural beauty. The southwestern corner of Uganda, including Kabale and Kisoro, have been described as a "little Switzerland," and deservedly so, with its crater lakes and meticulous terracing of the farmlands on the mountain slopes. The hills above Lake Bunyonyi offer a stunning view of crater lakes and islands, and the impenetrable forest near Kabale is the home of the Great Apes. Getting to within a few feet of the Silverback and watching these great creatures interact is a surreal experience.

The scenery of Uganda is varied. There are areas of long elephant grass; elsewhere endless papyrus swamps crisscross the country, while in other areas one can admire the order of the tea plantations. The road network is improving continuously, so that it's now possible to make the journey from Kampala to Fort Portal in the west in less than four hours on an excellent tarmac road, and one can drive all the way to Arua in West Nile on a newly built highway. Off the main roads, the red dirt roads stand in picturesque contrast to the green of the banana plantations, the elephant grass, the

coffee bushes, and the cassava or beans, all planted in small plots known as *shambas*.

CLIMATE

The climate is almost ideal year-round, with temperatures in the high seventies to low eighties Fahrenheit (high twenties Centigrade). Uganda lies on the Equator on a high plateau, with most of the country being at an elevation of 3,773 feet (1,150 m), rising to 4,921 feet (1,500 m) in the west, at Fort Portal and Kabale. It therefore has the advantage of having a tropical climate without the intense humidity one finds at the coast. The central region of Uganda around Kampala has temperatures with highs of 77–82°F (25–28°C) and lows of 60–64°F (16–18°C), and when one reaches the far west at Kabale and Fort Portal, or the eastern region at Sipi Falls and Mount Elgon, the temperature has highs of 77°F (25°C) and lows of 50–54°F (10–12°C). This is one of the few places in the world where one can see snow on the Equator.

There are two rainy seasons in the year—April to May, and September to November—but with the worldwide change in weather patterns, the rains are no longer predictable. Rains in Uganda are not monsoon-type rains lasting for days. Rain usually means heavy showers, which pass fairly quickly, and then the sun comes out and dries everything up. During the rainy season it usually rains at night or in the early morning, and it is an exception to have dull, overcast days. The north and the northeast of the country, particularly the Karamajong region, tend to be drier and have less dependable rains, with some years having complete drought and consequent food shortages. The temperature and the level of rainfall affect the life cycle of the mosquito, and therefore the malaria parasite, so the prevalence of malaria varies according to the temperature and whether it is a rainy or dry season.

CITIES AND TOWNS
Kampala
The capital city of Uganda is Kampala, with an official resident population of two million people, and a population in greater Kampala of three to four million. It is said to be a city set on seven hills, but has actually grown to cover at least ten. The city itself occupies a fairly small geographical area, with congestion being the word that springs to mind when one describes downtown Kampala. Many areas are densely populated, and the roads have simply become too small for the present-day volumes of traffic and people, though efforts are now

being made to create overpasses and bus lanes
to ease the flow.

Kampala could also be said to be a city that
never sleeps, since in certain areas the bars close
when the last customer goes home, while the
markets seem to do business from early morning
until late evening. Kampala is the home of the
national parliament, the Buganda Kingdom
parliament, the national museum, and the Kabakas'

tombs (the historic royal palace of the kings of Buganda, where several of the kings are now buried). The tombs were declared a UNESCO World Heritage Site in 2001, but, sadly, were partially destroyed by fire in 2010. Currently they are in the process of being rebuilt.

In a bid to ensure more long-term planning, the city was given priority for development, and central government put its management under the Office of the President, who appointed an executive director. The new administration has been able to make improvements in the roads, infrastructure, and general orderliness of the city, and has introduced some innovations, such as the Kampala Carnival (held in November), Christmas lights, and the planting of trees and shrubs.

Other Towns

There are several other large towns in Uganda, including Jinja in the east, at the source of the Nile, Entebbe in the southeast, where the airport is located, Gulu in the north, Mbarara in the west, Kabale in the southwest near the Rwanda border, and Fort Portal in the far west, near the Rwenzori Mountain range.

Jinja is popular for whitewater rafting on the Nile. Recently some of the rapids were submerged due to the construction of the long-awaited Bujagali Dam and hydro power plant, but other rapids farther up the river have been substituted, and rafting the Nile is still popular. Otherwise the pace of life in Jinja is less frenetic than that in Kampala, and many expatriates have chosen to settle here, sometimes building houses and hotels on the banks of the Nile, providing such leisure activities as horseback riding, quad biking, and bungee jumping—if such an activity can be considered leisurely.

Entebbe town and its airport are set on a peninsula of Lake Victoria. Entebbe Airport is where the famous "Raid on Entebbe" took place, and Entebbe is also home to the botanical gardens, with hundreds of species of trees, plus the Uganda Wildlife Education Centre. Off the shore is Ngambo Island, a sanctuary for abandoned chimpanzees. One can also set off from Entebbe for one of the many small Ssese Islands with which Lake Victoria is peppered. Some have hotels and tourist camps, and the largest have palm oil plantations.

Mbarara is a big town that mainly serves the farming community of this fertile area, but it also boasts a University of Science and Technology, so there is a large student population. Mbarara is a stop-off point for those traveling to the west, as well as being the largest town in the western part of Uganda. As such, it has a vibrant nightlife, though one has to know where to look. It may be something of a contradiction that the most "happening" place in town is a carwash; but this is true not only for Mbarara, but also for many other places in Uganda, where a daytime carwash mutates into a bar and disco in the evenings.

Fort Portal is set in beautiful farming country, where some early white settlers discovered the beauty and the fertility of both the land and the women! It is not uncommon to find mixed-race descendants in the Fort Portal area who can trace their ancestry back four or five generations to a white settler. There are beautiful tea plantations, set in spectacular scenery, and Kibale Forest nearby is also the home of the chimps, which can be trekked to on foot. Crater lakes in this area provide the backdrop for lodges and hotels perched precariously on ridges. Since Fort Portal is at a higher altitude than much of Uganda, it's cooler, making it suitable for tea plantations.

Kabale, in the southwest corner of the country, not far from the Rwanda border, has expanded rapidly, probably as a result of its proximity to Rwanda for trade, and also to Bwindi Impenetrable Forest, home to the gorillas. When one visits the crater lakes, such as Lake Bunyonyi, with their breathtaking beauty, one understands why Kabale is known as the "little Switzerland" of Uganda.

THE PEOPLE

The people of Uganda can be divided according to tribe, with over twenty tribes in existence. The dominant tribe is the Baganda. The Baganda (the people) occupy Buganda (the land) and speak Luganda (the language). When the early colonialists arrived in Buganda more than a century ago, they found that the Kingdom of Buganda had a well-organized hierarchy, under an absolute ruler, the Kabaka (King), and his court. The kingdom was divided into fifty-two clans, each with its elders and emblems. The totems of the clans can be seen on the walls of the Buganda Parliament in Mengo, Bulange.

What's in a Name?

Soon after I arrived in Uganda in 1987 I was adopted into the Kkobe clan. I was given the name Busulwa, which is a name distinctive to that clan, and more than a quarter of a century later I am still hailed in the street as Busulwa.

The totem for the Kkobe clan is Ekkobe Kaama, a climbing vine in the yam family that bears a fruit commonly referred to as an air potato. One of the rules of the clan is that you don't eat that which is your symbol: a plant or animal.

The legend of how my clan gained its totem goes as follows. A man once went to visit his in-laws and saw some good air potatoes on their land. Since there was a scarcity of food at his home he decided to help himself, and stole them for cooking and planting, hiding them in his goatskin bag at the roadside, where he was planning to pass the following morning. However, his in-laws escorted him beyond that point, so he had to leave the bag behind. On their way back the relatives saw his bag and found the air potatoes. They took them home, cooked them, and sent them to him. On realizing he had been discovered, he was dishonored, and committed suicide. His children refused to eat the thing that had caused their father's death, and from then on the air potato became their totem.

The British were impressed with the organization, administrative ability, and perceived superior intelligence of the Baganda people, and worked through the Buganda hierarchy to subjugate the rest of Uganda. However, they were not very sensitive to tribal sensibilities, and the borders they drew up cut through traditional tribal territories, so that some tribes cross the national boundaries between Uganda and Sudan, Kenya, and Rwanda. Some of the tribes of Uganda include the Banyankole (from the Ankole Kingdom) living in the southwest (Mbarara area), the Batoro from Fort Portal in the west (the Toro Kingdom), the Bakiga from Kabale in the far southwest, the Acholi from the north, the Langi from the northeast, the Madi straddling the border between Uganda and Sudan, the Itesots, the Basoga, and the Japadola from the east, and the Karamajong from the northeast. There are also many smaller tribes throughout the country.

Regional Differences

The colonialists tended to choose their civil servants from among the Baganda because they were seen as good administrators, while soldiers were recruited from the north as they were thought to be good fighters. Idi Amin was from the Kakwa tribe, which straddles the northern border with South Sudan (he was also the Ugandan national boxing champion). To this day, different tribes suffer from different stereotypes and it is often other tribes who highlight the caricatures. For example, the Bakiga have a reputation for determination, hard work, and intolerance of stupidity. This is probably because they come from Kabale, where the terrain is mountainous, and they are used to backbreaking work while attending to their crops on the mountainsides. The Banyankole, on the other hand, are from the western plains, where there is lush pasture for their cattle. Therefore, being pastoralists who tend to their cattle and drink milk, they have the reputation for being more laid back.

Some tribes had their own kings and royal families, and the early European explorers are reported to have been fascinated by the women of the Banyankole royal family because of their enormous backsides—even going to the trouble to take measurements. The Banyankole royal males were thought to have a preference for rounded, doe-eyed beauties, like the cattle they tended, and so the royal maidens were fattened on a diet of continuous milk drinking. Even today the women from that part of Uganda are very well endowed in the rear, though this can also be said of the Baganda women. Ugandan men are thought to like women who are well endowed, and don't go for skinny, Western-style beauty.

Ethnicity and Color

Ugandans are not slow to poke fun at each other, especially at the different tribes, colors, and accents that abound in this rich culture. While it may not be politically correct, and is even quite rude, to comment on the shape of someone's nose, or the way they pronounce their Ls and Rs, Ugandans can be merciless in mimicking each other. There are even professional comedians who mimic the President, with some being invited to functions with the "Big Man" himself present. Although, to the untrained ear, one may just hear a Ugandan accent, one soon realizes there are distinct differences in the pronunciation of Ugandan English and one can determine, as in most countries, whether a person comes from the north, south, east, or west of the country.

We tend to think in terms of Ugandans being black, since Uganda was a protectorate and not a colony and there are very few white settlers. However, there are also many shades and tones of black, with the darker-skinned people generally being from the hotter, northern parts of the country. It seems that everyone in the world wishes to gravitate to a common brown color, with whites damaging their skin in the sun in order to tan, while some Ugandans are prepared to use skin bleachers to make themselves lighter. In the end, the terms black and white are all relative, and beauty is in the eye of the beholder. What is striking about Ugandans is that no matter what their skin tone they are arguably the least racist people one could hope to meet. Ugandans are very secure in themselves, and if you accept them they will accept you.

The Baganda

The dominant tribe in Uganda has remained the Baganda to this day, because of their central location, their size, and their tendency to assimilate other tribes; one could say that there is "Bagandanization" of Uganda, though the subject of which tribe has political dominance is hotly debated. The lineage of the Baganda is paternal, so when a Muganda (singular for Baganda) man marries a woman from another tribe she is adopted into the Baganda tribe, and the offspring are Baganda. There are some who say that the lineage of the Kabaka is matriarchal, in that children take the clan of their mother and not the king, but traditionalists dispute this and say that the king has his own royal clan even though it has no totem. Offspring of the Kabaka must be from a Muganda wife in order to qualify as heir to the throne.

Ugandans' identity is both tribal and national: some will put their Ugandan nationality first and then their tribal identity, while others will put tribal identity first. There is no doubt that the Baganda have a very strong loyalty to their king, the Kabaka, since he embodies their long-held traditions. The Kabaka is revered, and in Buganda many official functions commence not only with the Ugandan national anthem but also with the Bugandan national anthem.

A BRIEF HISTORY

Uganda can trace its history to fifty thousand years ago with Paleolithic evidence of human activity on the shores of Lake Victoria, which was originally covered by dense rain forest. The forest was gradually cleared by Bantu-speaking agriculturalists, who by 400 BCE were forging iron tools and raising chickens, cattle, and goats. They displaced the indigenous hunter-gatherers to the mountains and settled in the area of the plateau north of Lake Victoria, while Nilotic pastoralists settled the areas west of the lake. Governance evolved gradually through clan leadership, which was used to organize labor, and ultimately evolved into the tribal structure that was well established by the nineteenth century.

Traditional Kingdoms

Uganda has four traditional kingdoms, two of which can trace their history back to the fourteenth century: the Buganda Kingdom in the south and Bunyoro Kingdom to the northwest. The Bunyoro Kingdom was in the ascendancy in the seventeenth

and eighteenth centuries, giving way to the Buganda Kingdom in the nineteenth century. The last five kings of Buganda are Mutesa I, followed by Mwanga II, Doudi Chwa II, Sir Edward Muteesa II, and the current king, Ronald Muwenda Mutebi I.

The Toro Kingdom in the west is an offshoot of the Bunyoro Kingdom, but did not come into being until 1822. The Ankole Kingdom in the southwest can also be traced back to the fifteenth century, when it was formed by the Bachwezi people from the legendary empire of the Kitara (there is debate as to whether this was a mythical or an actual empire) that spanned much of Uganda, Rwanda, northern Tanzania, and eastern Congo. The Ankole Kingdom had a centralized administration under the Omugabe (king). It was divided into two distinct castes: the Bahima, the nobility who were pastoralists, while the Bairu were peasants who lived by agriculture. The king was from the Bahima caste.

Ivory, Slaves, Guns, and Empire

During the mid-nineteenth century the first foreigners, in the form of Arab traders in search of slaves and ivory, arrived, bringing Islam with them. They were followed by Catholic and Protestant missionaries, bringing their own religious rivalry, and then by European traders and arms dealers. The British, who had originally intended to run Uganda through a commercial company, the Imperial British East Africa Company, found that they needed to use the full weight of the Empire to establish effective control. They were facilitated in this by the outbreak of the religious civil wars (1888–92) and the fact that Captain Frederick Lugard of the Company was the only party to the conflict with a maxim gun.

The first missionaries to arrive were the Protestants under the British Church Missionary Society (CMS) in 1877, and the Catholic White Fathers from France in 1879. When Mwanga II attempted to outlaw the various religious factions he was deposed in 1888, and a religious war followed between the Muslims and the Christians in which the Muslims at first triumphed, but were then defeated by the alliance of Christians. However, this alliance itself then fragmented, with the Protestants supporting the British claim for control under Captain Lugard, while the Catholics supported the German claim under Karl Peters. In this case Lugard had the biggest gun and the Catholics were defeated,

with the burning down of the Catholic mission in 1892. In 1894 Britain established a protectorate over Buganda and two years later over Ankole, Bunyoro, and Toro.

Alongside these developments the matter of "settling the Nile"—finding the source of the great River Nile—had long intrigued the members of the British Royal Geographical society in the nineteenth century, leading to many expeditions by Europeans

and at least one American looking for fame and fortune. Perhaps the best-known early explorer was Dr. David Livingstone, who was more motivated by spreading the Christian Gospel than by the desire for conquest, but his very presence in East Africa precipitated several other expeditions, not only to find him, but to identify the source of the Nile. Some of the well-known names, John Speke, Henry Morton Stanley, Richard Burton, Emin Pasha, and Gordon of Khartoum, have received extensive historical coverage in this fascinating period of European history.

These early forays into East Africa in general, and Uganda in particular, resulted in the dividing up of the continent among the colonial powers in "the scramble for Africa," with Uganda falling within the British sphere of influence. However, the early administrators of Uganda argued for, and achieved, a different form of government from that in neighboring Kenya, where white settlers were encouraged to immigrate to the Kenya highlands. In the case of Uganda it was recognized that it was preferable to rule Uganda through its existing structures, and thus Uganda remained a protectorate.

Colonial Rule to Independence, 1894–1962

One outcome of this status was that, apart from a
few notables in the Fort Portal area, there were
very few white settlers in Uganda. It is likely that
this history has resulted in Ugandans themselves
being far less fixated on their colonial history than
other African countries. Ugandans also have zero
sense of inferiority, and total confidence in their
own identity.

The British preserved the various kingdoms and
worked through them in a model of indirect rule, so
that when Uganda gained independence in October
1962, the Kabaka of Buganda was designated

the president,
and the leader
of the largest
political party
(the left-wing
Uganda People's
Congress), Dr.
Milton Obote,
became prime
minister.

The Pearl Of Africa

Winston Churchill visited Uganda and wrote a book in 1908 entitled *My African Journey*, in which he wrote: "For magnificence, for variety of form and color, for profusion of brilliant life—bird, insect, reptile, beast—for vast scale—Uganda is truly 'the Pearl of Africa.' The Kingdom of Uganda is a fairy tale. The scenery is different, the climate is different and most of all, the people are different from anything elsewhere to be seen in the whole range of Africa . . . what message I bring back . . . concentrate upon Uganda."

After Churchill's comment there were high hopes for Uganda's continued development. Sadly this was not to be, as within a few years tensions grew between the socialist-leaning prime minister and the Kabaka, which ended with the prime

minister and parliament abolishing the kingdoms and the role of the Kabaka as president, abrogating this role to the prime minister. Hence the kingdoms that had survived British rule were abolished in 1967 under the post-colonial administration.

Idi Amin, 1971–79

It was during the regime of President Obote that Idi Amin was elevated to the position of head of the army, and when Obote left the country for a conference in 1971 Amin used the opportunity to seize power in a military coup. At first he had widespread support from the population, and indeed the former colonial powers, since he was not seen as a threat. Moreover Obote's rule had become increasingly oppressive, and he had alienated himself from the Baganda by attacking the palace and forcing the Kabaka into exile But the picture rapidly changed as Amin purged all who were threats, or perceived threats, to his position. His bloody reign continued to be marked by a mixture of comedy and tragedy, since he was able to hold the world stage by his amusing commentary on international events, while at the same time continuing to eliminate anyone who put their head above the parapet.

Titles Idi Amin Gave Himself

"His Excellency, President for Life, Field Marshal Al Hadji Doctor Idi Amin Dada, VC, DSO, MC, Lord of All the Beasts of the Earth and Fishes of the Seas, and Conqueror of the British Empire in Africa in General and Uganda in Particular."

For some people the only thing they know about Uganda is the name Idi Amin, yet it is now more than thirty-five years since he cast his shadow over the country. After being ousted by the Tanzanian army he continued to live a long life in exile in Saudi Arabia, and died at a ripe old age as a very fat man in 2003. Today Uganda has long since moved on from the era of Amin, but one cannot get away from the damage that he did to the country, not just in terms of its image.

Expulsion of the Asians
Amin was responsible for the expulsion of more than sixty thousand Ugandan Asians, who in 1972 were forced to leave without most of their worldly possessions in the so-called "Ugandanization" of private businesses.

Ugandans had been categorized into certain classes by their colonial masters. Uganda's Asians were seen as the class that could do business in a way in which the "natives" were not capable. The result was that while most indigenous black Ugandans mainly worked on the land, the entrepreneurial Asians, who had originally come to East Africa to build the railway line, were the traders and factory operators and owners, typically in cotton ginning or coffee husking. Thus, when the Asians were thrown out of the country there was little expertise and capital to continue these essential businesses, leading to a collapse of the private sector and the shrinking of the economy by 20 percent.

After eight years of inept, brutal rule by Amin, in which tens of thousands of people were murdered, the country was "liberated" by the Tanzanian army in 1979. This led to looting and further hardship for the people, since the Tanzanian army lived off the spoils of the land. After a further period of two years, in which there were a number of interim presidents, general elections were held and Milton Obote, the leader

of the Uganda People's Congress, and the previous
president, was declared the winner.

Civil War, 1981–86

Unfortunately the elections in December 1980
were not seen as free and fair. Yoweri Museveni,
who was the minister of defense in the interim
government, refused to accept the results and,
with twenty-seven men, went back to the bush
to start a resistance movement. Thus another war
was fought between 1982 and 1986 in the bush
of the Luweero Triangle, just north of Kampala,
in which it is estimated that three hundred
thousand people perished. Toward the end of
1986 the Obote regime disintegrated in
internecine fighting and Museveni's National
Resistance Army (NRA) was able to take
advantage of its weakness and marched
victoriously into Kampala.

Joseph Kony and the Lord's Resistance Army

Although the National Resistance Movement
brought peace to most of the country, including
the central, western, and eastern areas, the Acholi
north continued to be terrorized by the rebel
Lord's Resistance Army (LRA) for another
twenty years, until its leader, Joseph Kony, was
finally driven from the country in 2008.

Kony, a lay reader in the Anglican Church, was
from a village in Acholiland in the north of the
country, which had a reputation for being steeped
in witchcraft and having a particularly powerful
shrine. He was influenced by a mixture of religion
and superstition, which found fertile ground in
the delusions of his paranoid schizophrenic

personality and gave him justification (in his own mind) for his actions. This has made him one of the most dangerous sociopaths that Africa, or the world, has ever known. Kony has been directly responsible for the deaths of tens of thousands of people, many of them children.

When the NRA took over Kampala, more than twenty-five years ago, the remnants of the old national army were disbanded, but a few hardened criminals and soldiers fled north, and although the bulk of them were subdued (many soldiers being retrained and absorbed into the ranks of the NRA), there was a remnant that never surrendered and stayed in the far reaches of northern Uganda to foment trouble.

One of their more colorful leaders was a lady named Alice Lakwena, who led the "Holy Spirit Movement" and assured her followers that when they were anointed with her oil of the Holy Spirit (which was shea butter), the bullets of the army would bounce off. Thus her followers went into battle to discover, to their personal cost, that their leader's words were more powerful than her magic and they were not in fact bulletproof.

This movement thus fizzled out, but Joseph Kony, a cousin of Alice Lakwena, felt that he had a more powerful communication from "the Angels" and took up the campaign. He was joined by the hardened veterans from the previous regime, and his movement became known as the Lord's Resistance Army, because Kony believed that Uganda should be ruled by the Ten Commandments. His movement would have died out, but he adopted the strategy of kidnapping children and brutalizing them so that they obeyed his commands without question. There was thus plenty of fodder for his army since there was no shortage of children in the villages, which he constantly raided, burning homes, killing the parents, and abducting the children. The abductees were then made to endure horrors, such as killing their friends and sometimes even their own families. Anyone who was caught trying to escape was killed, usually by being beaten to death. The boys who had been captured became "rebels," and the girls were made to do hard labor in the fields and were given to his commanders as sex slaves.

There were times when the Ugandan army appeared to be on the brink of capturing Kony and crushing his movement, but the situation was delicate, since Kony was always surrounded by those whom he had abducted. The "rebels" who were burning villages, looting, and killing were almost all children who had been abducted. The army adopted the strategy of denying the LRA food, and the opportunity to capture more children, by forcing the northern population to live in internally displaced person's camps (IDPs). There were tens of thousands of people in these camps, who could not get to their *shambas* to plant crops and who were forced into a life of idleness, waiting for the next consignment of food and handouts from the international relief agencies. To add to their misery, there was always the risk of being attacked by the LRA, since the

rebels would still regularly target the IDP camps and kill the inhabitants, despite the presence of the army. Tens of thousands of children were abducted over a period of fifteen years, many horrendous massacres were carried out, and as years became decades, many believed that the government and the army did not have the political will to finish the insurgency off. Whether this was the case (or whether the army simply lacked the training and logistics), there was a lingering suspicion that the people of the north were being punished for their association with the army of Milton Obote during the previous regime.

During the period of "Obote Two," when Museveni and the NRA were fighting a guerrilla campaign in Luwero between 1982 and 1986, several hundred thousand people were killed. The soldiers of Obote's army were drawn mainly from the Acholi in the north, and the words "Acholi" and "soldier" were interwoven. Thus, when Luweero and the central region gained peace, and an insurgency broke out in the north, among

some there was a tacit feeling that they were now getting their just rewards. Of course this was in no way institutionalized, but there was an underlying assumption throughout the north that people from other parts of Uganda simply didn't care.

In the end, through increased military efficiency, the LRA were chased from northern Uganda and peace was restored, but to this day Joseph Kony roams the forests of the Central African Republic, wreaking havoc on the local population, and it now appears that the "International Community" doesn't have the capacity to stop the misery he is causing to the innocent. Northern Uganda is now entirely peaceful. Gulu is a thriving, bustling town, with a heavy cross-border trade with South Sudan.

PRESENT-DAY POLITICS

Since 1986 the president has been Yoweri Kaguta Museveni, now the longest-serving president in East Africa. The ruling party is the National Resistance Movement (NRM), which has dominated politics in Uganda for more than twenty-seven years. Although Ugandans were very satisfied with the accomplishments of the NRM during their first two decades in power, there has been more dissent since the constitution was amended, through a referendum in 2005, to allow a president to serve more than two terms. However, since the opposition was weak, Yoweri Museveni has continued in office through the electoral process. Ugandans are aware of their troubled post-colonial history and value peace and stability—which, despite other shortcomings, President Museveni has continued to deliver.

GOVERNMENT

The form of government is a presidential republic with a multiparty parliamentary democracy and an independent judiciary. The president is directly elected for a term of five years and is head of state, the army, and

the government. There is a one-chamber parliament that passes legislation, which is then assented to by the president. The judiciary consists of magistrates' courts, the High Court, the Court of Appeal, and the Constitutional Court. Elections are held at the same time every five years for the office of the president, MPs, district chairmen and mayors of municipalities, and councilors and local government politicians.

"Balancing the Cabinet"

Cabinet members are appointed by the president and can be chosen from sitting members of parliament or from business or the professions. As well as full ministers, there are a large number of "ministers of state," making a cabinet of seventy people. The reason for this high number is for "balancing," because the electorate, from different tribes and regions of the country, wish to feel that they have one of their own in cabinet. This is the politics of representation by an elite, where a small number of people are given privileged positions in return for keeping the masses loyal to the party. While the system is widely practiced in many countries, there is a high price tag in the cost of keeping a large number of cabinet ministers on the public payroll. Thus a hefty proportion of the budget goes into public administration, rather than the development of long-term infrastructure.

This philosophy of governance is in sharp contrast to that of neighboring Rwanda, where development and service delivery are aimed directly at the electorate, with politicians and public servants being set strict targets. If they fail, they either resign or have a lot of explaining to do to their constituents.

Elections

Elections are always hotly contested, with many candidates spending large sums of money on their campaigns. There is a general perception that election campaigns offer one of the few opportunities for the electorate to benefit directly from their politicians, and although there are laws against giving handouts or other such inducements, the practice is nevertheless widespread. Gifts in kind are given, such as soap and sugar, as well as cash benefits. There is, of course, no guarantee that just because a candidate spreads his money around he will be elected.

Apart from the direct benefits that the aspiring politician may give to his electorate, there are also the substantial costs of these relatively long campaigns, in terms of transport, posters, and campaign rallies. Politics is not for the fainthearted, and there are many wealthy individuals who have gone broke in their pursuit of a political career. The flip side of this kind of campaigning is that there is a 70 percent turnover of parliamentarians in every parliament. Obviously the sitting politician should have an advantage, so either there was a noticeable lack of performance resulting in disenchantment, or a wealthier candidate came along, with deeper pockets and more grandiose promises.

The Electoral Process
It has been said that the normal multiparty Western democratic system does not really work in a poor country because poor people have a different hierarchy of needs from those living in a stable, well-off society. In Uganda there are loud complaints by the opposition after every election about the fairness of the system, and many of these complaints are justified. What one must bear in mind is that the elections are simply a reflection of the state of the society as a whole. It is impossible to get an election up to American or European standards when it is conducted by officials who measure themselves by an entirely different yardstick. Despite this, there is an articulate and vocal opposition that makes its presence felt, especially in the media and on the streets.

THE ECONOMY
Population Growth
Uganda has a high fertility rate and a yearly increase of population of 3.1 percent—almost the highest in the world. The fertility rate (the average number of pregnancies per woman in her lifetime) of Ugandan women is 5.9. The high birth rate is due in part to complicated sexual networking, particularly among the poor, where a woman may be a serial monogamist and therefore have children to more than one man throughout her life, while a man may father children simultaneously from

more than one wife. Traditionally, children have been valued as an informal social protection system for one's old age, and men were seen as more powerful according to the number of children they had fathered. In contrast, today middle-class Ugandans limit the numbers of their offspring as they are aware of their financial and educational responsibilities toward their children.

This high number of children has resulted in a situation in which each working person is supporting a large number of dependants. The demographic shift should mean that when these children are educated they will become a skilled labor resource for the country. Unfortunately the education system is not as strong as it should be, and the outcome may be a large number of young people without jobs. This may lead to unrest, unless jobs are created and young people are trained with appropriate skills.

The Agricultural and Oil Sectors

Eighty percent of Ugandans live in rural areas, making their livelihood from agriculture—mainly subsistence farming, since there are very few large commercial farms. This is to some extent due to

the prevailing land laws, where ownership of land is complex, and it is difficult for potential commercial farmers to find large tracts of land without encumbrance. On the other hand, 70 percent of Uganda's GDP is generated within Kampala, which houses the headquarters of all the banks, the large businesses, the embassies, and the NGOs. Hence, although Uganda is still a largely peasant economy, a high rate of development is taking place in the urban areas, especially Kampala.

Over the next decade Uganda will become an oil-producing country, since oil has been discovered in relatively large quantities in the Lake Albert basin. The industry will move from exploration to extraction and refining within the next five years. The development of this sector has been slow, due mainly to delays in putting in place the legislative framework and to the slow pace of work within the public sector. The oil sector provides the opportunity for huge development of the economy in transport, logistics, infrastructure, and scaling-up of skills in trades such as welding, steel fabrication, carpentry, electrical skills, and plumbing. The challenge is for Uganda to prepare adequately for this windfall, otherwise the jobs will go to expatriates and nationals from surrounding East African countries.

Telecoms and Banking

In Uganda, as in many other African countries, there has been an explosion in the telecoms sector, with big players such as Airtel, Orange, and MTN dominating the market. The result of this mobile telephony has been that Uganda has leapfrogged into the twenty-first century in terms of communication, and that every remote corner of the country is now connected.

The formalization of banking has also been another significant step forward for the country, with a strong central bank that controls inflation and regulates industry. Microfinance organizations have also grown into banks in their own right, with banks such as Equity Bank and Centenary Bank providing banking to the grassroots community and the hitherto unbanked population. Mobile money—the ability to transfer money through cell phones—is developing as another grassroots banking facility and as the means of transferring cash cheaply.

Economic Outlook

The IMF rates Uganda as a stable economy, maintaining economic indicators within acceptable levels, and managing public borrowing. However, in 2013, as the Ministry of Finance sought to tighten controls in the public sector, there was a

noticeable reduction in the awarding of private contracts by government, which in turn affected the rate of economic activity, as the government is the largest customer of the private sector. Following the unearthing of a large scam in the Office of the Prime Minister, some high-level civil servants were arrested and the government was forced by donors to introduce increased accountability, checks, and balances. The net effect should ultimately be to stem corruption.

Development of Infrastructure

Uganda has maintained a healthy economic growth rate of 5–10 percent for the last two decades. Bottlenecks, such as the shortage of electricity generation, are being addressed with the long-awaited commissioning of the Bujagali Hydroelectric project and the commencement of the Karuma Falls hydro-electric dam. The EU favors a policy of government borrowing for infrastructure development, supported by the EU's paying the interest on such loans until oil comes on stream. China has also been actively involved, both in buying into the oil sector and in supporting Chinese contractors carrying out infrastructure projects. Such private finance initiatives are welcome, provided there is transparency.

Uganda is at somewhat of a disadvantage, being a landlocked country many hundreds of miles from the nearest port. However, recent negotiations in the newly re-formed East African Community have seen agreement for the building of a new railway link to the coast, and the removal of non-tariff barriers (such as weighbridges and other checks, causing delays for commercial traffic), which should ensure cheaper and faster transport of goods from the coast. Rwanda is a member of the East African Community and, with Uganda, has been lobbying for lower costs and increased efficiency in transport.

On the other hand, Uganda's landlocked status can work for it in terms of being located centrally in the region. If it developed more commercial farming projects, Uganda could become the breadbasket of East Africa. Some manufacturing facilities, such as steel smelting and steel rolling mills, have set up in the country, and from there have established markets in the DRC, South Sudan, Rwanda, Western Kenya, and Burundi. Organizations such as Mukwano Industries, which make a variety of products from detergents to plastics for the local market, have a complete manufacturing and distribution system, not only to the rural areas of Uganda but to the surrounding countries.

The Education Business

Uganda has, historically, a good reputation for secondary and tertiary education, mainly because Makerere University was the foremost university in East Africa in pre- and post-colonial times. Unfortunately, due to the political instability the country suffered under the Amin and Obote Two regimes, the university fell behind in research and academic standards. However, recently it has climbed back in the ratings and is seeking to establish itself again as a center of academic excellence and research. This good reputation for education appears to have put Uganda on the map in terms of secondary and tertiary education institutions, and there is an influx of students from surrounding countries, resulting in a proliferation of

secondary schools and private universities. The fact that the fees are lower in Uganda than in the rest of the region is also a significant draw for regional students. Unfortunately in some cases teaching is not up to international standards, with some institutions being more interested in attracting a high number of students than maintaining strict academic standards. There are many courses in the "chalk and talk" subjects, such as social sciences and law, producing large numbers of graduates, but there are insufficient students graduating in scienctific subjects such as engineering and medicine, where there are real shortages of qualified workers and opportunities for employment.

THE LEGAL SYSTEM

The legal system is based on the British model. The judiciary consists of magistrates' courts, commercial courts, the High Court, the Appeal Court, and the Constitutional Court. There have been instances in which magistrates have been bribed, but this is much less likely at the level of the High Court or beyond. In fact, it is not their Lordships who can be bribed, but lower-level officials who can be induced to do such things as "misplacing" files. Generally speaking the judiciary is independent and can be trusted, though it may take some time for the processes of law to work their way through the courts, since the judiciary has been understaffed.

Uganda produces more than a thousand lawyers a year, compared to fewer than two hundred medical doctors. Those with a British law degree can practice in Uganda provided they pass the one-year course of the Law Development Centre.

UGANDA IN AFRICA

Uganda is part of the East African Community and of the African Union. It has a well-trained army that has been instrumental (as part of the African Union) in bringing a semblance of order to Somalia. Uganda plays a key role in regional stability and has an influence on the Democratic Republic of Congo, South Sudan, and Somalia. President Museveni, as the longest-serving leader in East Africa, is a power broker, and has been useful to American foreign policy in curbing the influence of radical Islamic fundamentalist groups beyond the Horn of Africa. The Ugandan army (UPDF) is relatively well organized and disciplined and has contributed heavily to African Union forces.

In commercial terms Uganda is a lightweight compared to Kenya, with little economic punching power. Even so, it is a critical player in the East African community, not only because President Museveni is the elder statesman, but also because Uganda has a unique position in the Great Lakes region. President Kagame of Rwanda was a protégé of Museveni, although he has long since grown beyond this role. President Salva Kier of South Sudan is highly dependent on Uganda, and President Kabila of the DRC has only recently been able to drive his motorcade through the eastern region of DRC, which, to many, is seen more naturally as coming under a Ugandan and Rwandan sphere of influence. Uganda was involved in brokering a peace deal between the DRC and the rebel movement M23, and has also been active as a peace broker in the conflict between the Nuer and the Dinka in South Sudan.

chapter **two**

VALUES & ATTITUDES

THE UGANDAN CHARACTER

Of course it is impossible to generalize on the character of over thirty million people, but the remark is often made that Ugandans are friendly, and it is the case that most Ugandans are happy to start up a conversation with a stranger. Riding on a bus in Uganda is a very different experience from riding on the London Underground: people are curious, and will want to know about you. Even though the official language is English, many of the local people are not fluent in it, which can make communication more difficult but by no means impossible. The level of spoken English is more widespread than in either Kenya or Tanzania, so it is not hard to find your way around, or communicate reasonably well, even if you are deep in the country. Ugandans can also be very empathetic, but may be shy to demonstrate this side to foreigners.

Sense of Humor

As in any other nation, there is a whole range of character types, but if one is open and inclusive in Uganda, it is easy to form relationships, exchange a joke or a story, and be accepted by the society.

Ugandans have a good sense of humor and will laugh uproariously, particularly at slapstick comedy, and even though some jokes may get lost in translation there is usually something to laugh about. The nuances of sarcasm and satire may not be readily understood, though in Kampala among the middle classes and on the radio stations one will find these forms of humor. The stand-up comic routine was unknown until recently, but now there are a number of comedians, both in English and the vernacular, who are side-splittingly funny.

Ugandans were rated as the happiest people in East Africa, according to a recent UN report on happiness. The report concluded that it was not because of their physical circumstances, which were often adverse, but because of their outlook on life, and their appreciation of the little they have. There are many poor people in Uganda who don't know where the next meal is coming from, but this does not stop them having fun or cracking a joke. Laughter is a big part of the society and, although there is often much to be sorrowful about in the harshness and rawness of life, people will generally see the funny side of things. Perhaps it is this irrepressible sense of humor that keeps people going in the direst of circumstances.

Faith

A characteristic that sometimes mystifies Europeans is the deep-seated religious belief of many Ugandans. Sometimes this seems to be misplaced in a "dodgy" pastor or a flamboyant

American evangelist, but it is often a simple
faith in God that keeps people going. There are
those whose deep-rooted faith in God sees them
through the most adverse circumstances. It may
be difficult for people from more secular societies
to sort out the wheat from the chaff, in that there
appear to be so many charlatans in the business
of religion, but one should not be blinded by this
superficial manifestation of religion. There are a
significant number of deeply religious people
whose faith is very real—including the wife of the
president, who is a serious "born-again" believer.
While there are those whose spirituality may not

be related to a
particular
religion, most
people are
devout Catholics,
Protestants,
or Muslims.
Spirituality in
Uganda has more
often than not
become equated
with formal
religion, and
there is little of
the mystical search for spiritual meaning that one
may find, for example, in an ashram in India.

Being Polite
Many Ugandans don't like any kind of
confrontation or saying "no," since they feel this is
rude, so they will gauge what they think you want

and agree with you. The problem is that they may not actually understand what you are saying at all, but are too polite to say so, therefore, when you ask them if they understand, they will just say yes. If you are not sure that someone understands you, ask him or her to repeat what you have said, which will give them the opportunity to let you know that they haven't understood your accent. Bear in mind that the word "please" does not exist in the local language, which results either in the non-use of the word, with someone appearing abrupt, or the overuse of it, by someone saying "Thank you, please," because they don't understand how it should be used.

Weighing the Evidence

Despite the efforts of the government to provide universal primary education, the majority of Ugandans are still poorly educated by Western standards, with little real comprehension of scientific theory or scientific proof. And because many people are either unemployed or under-employed, there is plenty of time for storytelling, which historically has been a major pastime since Uganda has a long oral tradition. However, like a good Hollywood movie, the facts may become somewhat incidental, so long as the story is interesting and adheres to generally held beliefs.

This form of folklore has influenced the standards of certain media outlets, including local radio stations and some sections of the print media. The unique combination of "tabloid" reporting mixed with a folkloric approach can result in widely circulated stories that are actually opinions and may have little factual basis (not so different from some sections of Western media). Where there are scientifically and factually presented arguments, the less educated may have difficulty in making a judgment as to what is true and what is false, and so will simply comment, "so they say." An example of this attitude is the belief in witchcraft, as opposed to modern medicine. Witchcraft is often tried first, and the patient is taken to the hospital only when his condition deteriorates. Of course if the patient then dies in the hospital, this simply confirms that modern medicine does not work.

Tall Tales

At one time the story went around that there was no point in using condoms because they had been shown to have small holes that allowed particles as large as ground pepper to get through. As a result, condoms were perceived as useless in protecting against the HIV virus and were discarded. The pepper story did the rounds, yet I never did find the brave person who demonstrated the pepper effect.

GENDER ROLES

There is a high representation of women in parliament, and many women are in influential positions in the country, but on the other hand Ugandan society could be described as chauvinistic.

Many Ugandan men like to have their wives or girlfriends totally dependent on them. Traditionally, men went out to work, while the women stayed at home to cook and work in the *shamba*, and some villagers still feel very insecure if  their wife has an independent livelihood. It is common to hear complaints from such men about their wives being "proud" because of their newly found independence. Submission is highly valued in traditional society, which still influences present-day values. Women were supposed to submit to their husbands in practically everything, from welcoming him back in the proper manner after returning from work, to having his food prepared, to managing the household, and pleasing him in bed. Girls were taught how to please their man in every department, from the kitchen to the bedroom.

While many girls brought up in the city do not adhere to this kind of role and are altogether more enlightened, it is interesting that they are still happy to let the man buy the drinks or pay for the meal when they are out socializing. There are very few girls who feel the necessity of "going Dutch," and even if they did make the suggestion, the man would generally not hear of it. It seems there is still a macho persona for men, who must continue to give the appearance of being the provider, even in today's modern world. In the final analysis it all revolves around money: the man is expected to have the money to provide for the needs of the woman, and, if he is dating, he must show that he has some financial clout. The combination of modern values and tradition produces a unique mixture of modernity and dependence for women.

In the commercial world it is noticeable that many women have risen to middle and senior level management positions, and a few have now reached the top, as managing directors of banks. This is partly because women are prepared to rise steadily within the company, while many

Ugandan men appear to be too impatient to wait for progress on the corporate ladder and thus leave for more entrepreneurial activities. Sometimes the lure of quick and easy money in a deal is too hard to resist.

ATTITUDES TOWARD HOMOSEXUALITY

Homosexuality was already illegal in Uganda under colonial-era laws. However, the recent passing of the Anti-Homosexuality Act, proposing life imprisonment for same-sex relations, has given the country a poor international image. There is a difference between public and private attitudes, and living here it is hard to feel that Uganda is a repressive country. It is normally a case of "live and let live," but there has been a noticeable shift in attitude regarding gay rights of late.

The intolerance toward gays derives to some extent from a reaction to international organizations that are seen as promoting a "gay lobby." There is, of course, no evidence for such a lobby, and in fact there is a misperception regarding international organizations that are concerned about basic human rights. Many Ugandans (and indeed Africans) feel that they are being told how to behave and that this is an imposition on their traditional culture and values. Although they acknowledge the existence of homosexuality in their societies, they feel threatened that Western organizations are seeking to promote it.

The anti-gay bill has been generally supported because it is seen as protecting Ugandan family values. Sadly the debate about human rights was misunderstood as an attempt to impose the right of those with a homosexual orientation to "recruit" among Ugandan young people. Many Ugandans who were in favor of the bill did not think through the human rights issues involved.

It is also the case that many do not understand the reasons behind homosexuality, and take the simplistic view that sexual orientation is a choice. When international condemnation rained down on Uganda, many felt that the very fabric of Ugandan culture was being attacked.

The anti-gay lobby in Uganda is also fueled by Evangelicals, mainly from the USA, who see Africa as the place for the Church to make its last stand against the "evils" of the gay movement. It has, therefore, been relatively easy for the anti-gay lobby to gain traction in the guise of fighting for the preservation of African values. Historically, homosexuals have always been accepted and tolerated as part of society, but the recent anti-gay bill has meant that many are keeping a low profile, while some have quietly left the country.

The Kabaka's Favorites

The paradox is that homosexuality is well known in the history of Buganda: the last international incident, which took place in the late nineteenth century, was when the Kabaka Mwanga II burned a number of his court page boys at the stake because they had converted to Christianity and refused to join in his homosexual activities.

DRESS SENSE

Ugandans sometimes feel that Westerners are unkempt, particularly when they see backpackers walking down the street wearing flip-flops, shorts, and dirty T-shirts. As a generalization, Ugandans dress very well, and women in the cities are aware of the latest fashions. Tight jeans are ubiquitous, both for casual dress and for nightclubs. Short skirts are best reserved for clubs and pubs. Recently parliament passed an anti-pornography law that was dubbed "the mini-skirt bill," since it banned showing sexually provocative parts of the body, including thighs. The bill has become the subject of numerous jokes on the airwaves, and the length of skirts has not increased.

In the villages, women generally dress modestly, and it is respectful not to wear skimpy shorts, though trousers are acceptable. In the cities, most ways of dressing are acceptable, but if a woman wears something skimpy or short in the bus park or the market, she can expect to be sexually harassed, and men will make rude remarks in Luganda (at which point it is best not to understand what they are saying).

THE EXTENDED FAMILY

The extended family is a well-known institution in Africa, and, simply put, it means that the family is not confined to the nuclear family of father, mother, and 2.5 children, but can include aunts and uncles, grandparents, children of a deceased relative, and needy distant relatives who have been taken into the household. In the West the concept of adoption is of a very formal procedure, with serious legal implications, and the sense that a child who is adopted has equal status to other, biological, children. In Uganda the attitude to taking another child into the family is much more relaxed, and there may be no formalities involved. Such children may be the offspring of a distant relative who has died of HIV, or the dependants of a friend who cannot support them. The extended family is the informal social network that the country depends on in the absence of any national social security schemes. The advent of AIDS has meant that no family has been left unaffected, either through losing relatives or taking in those left without support.

Although there are social workers and court procedures for both fostering and adoption, they are absolutely overstretched, and much of this activity is carried out on an informal basis. Without the extended family it is difficult to see how Africa would survive. There are no old peoples' homes in Uganda, though it would be the ideal place to grow old, with lots of people to look after you. Old people are respected, and elders are looked after by the family and the village. It's like that well-known saying, "It takes a village to bring up a child," meaning that in the traditional village setting everyone has responsibility for bringing up the children.

RESPECT FOR ELDERS, AND OBEDIENCE
To some extent the old adage "Children should be seen and not heard" still applies in Uganda. Children are taught to be well behaved, and to

greet their elders when they come into a room, but not to be too forward. Many Ugandans who have the opportunity to send their children to school abroad do not like the values that a foreign education inculcates in them. They say that the child has become "stubborn," meaning that their child is less compliant with traditions and more ready to speak up for himself. While it is normal for a parent to wish to have respectful children, teaching passivity also has the adverse effect of producing adults without inquiring minds. In the worst examples, the children are well behaved, but simply regurgitate what they are taught in class, which is often flawed. On the whole Ugandan teachers do not tolerate dissent and do not stand for questioning of what is being spoon-fed to the students.

SEXUAL NETWORKING AND HIV

Due to the advent of HIV there have been many campaigns to promote faithfulness and monogamy, particularly the ABC campaign: Abstain, Be faithful, or use a Condom. There was much made of "zero grazing": stay at home with your spouse, and don't look for greener pastures. Recently there has also been a campaign advising people to avoid the "sexual network"—something like a virtual London Underground. This is based on the recognition that although Uganda, being a modern society, embraces monogamy as the accepted norm, it is very common for men to have other relationships. These are often referred to as "side wives," or "side dishes."

Women are also free to move to another man if the husband has not formalized the commitment. Thus we have a variety of sexual networks, with men being informally polygamous, while the women may be serially monogamous, particularly in rural areas. The result is a very complex sexual network. Traditionally it was easy to identify a polygamous family, and there was a certain order to it; now it is more difficult to know how many children a man or woman has, or which relationships he or she is in. This has resulted in the spread of HIV, and although the prevalence of HIV has now reduced, the incidence (the number of new cases) is on the increase. The prevalence in the general population is just under 7 percent.

CHRISTIANITY, ISLAM, ANIMISM, AND RELIGIOUS TOLERATION

All religions in Uganda have a degree of syncretism, having been influenced by traditional Kiganda beliefs that predate Islam and Christianity. The belief that everything, whether animate or inanimate, possesses a soul or spirit is the earliest form of religion. All parts of nature have a soul. and humans are considered part of nature, not separate from it; there is no separation of the material and spiritual realms.

This animist world view gave rise to the Kiganda religion, with its belief in a supreme deity known as Katonda. He was represented by about thirty Balubaale (singular Lubaale), demi-gods or hero-saints, who had power over certain areas of the universe, such as rain or fertility. There are many well-known shrines to the various Balubaale and to the lesser spirits of departed ancestors at community and household level. These are tended by a clan member who will become "possessed" from time to time. Various sacrifices and rituals were required to communicate with or appease the deities.

Uganda was a fertile, civilized land compared to some of the tribal areas that surrounded it, and so was a preferred destination for those wishing to bring their own brand of civilization, trade, or religion. Christianity was introduced by the early missionaries, who also brought with them the division between Catholic and Protestant. Islam was introduced by Arab traders and slavers who descended on Uganda from the coast and from Egypt.

Although there have been religious wars within the past 120 years, and some political parties are identified with one or other religion, Ugandans are generally tolerant, with different religions co-existing side by side. Some families have a Muslim branch and a Christian branch, depending on intermarriage, while it is not unusual for young people from the Catholic Church to attend more lively Pentecostal churches, without abandoning their Catholicism. The Ugandan brand of Islam is generally tolerant, and it is only recently that there have been jihadist-type actions, mainly associated with Al Shabab in Somalia. Few Muslim women cover themselves completely in the black *hijab*, though many wear brightly colored headdresses.

ATTITUDES TOWARD TIME

Ugandans generally have a more relaxed attitude to time than you might be used to. Times for appointments and organized events can be somewhat elastic. Ugandans themselves now ask, "Do you mean *mzungu* time or Ugandan time?" If it is *mzungu* (white man's) time then you aim for the time you have been told; if it is Ugandan time you can allow a margin, depending on the event. A wedding reception will be around two hours late, though the wedding service may be on time, since it has to fit into the church's timetable. A business meeting in the public sector could be one hour late, but is generally on time in the formal private sector. An invitation to meet for a drink in the evening at eight could mean any time after that.

ATTITUDES TOWARD WORK

Uganda is richly endowed with natural resources. These include water, thanks to abundant rainfall, with many rivers and waterfalls that can be used for the generation of electricity. There are two wet seasons, and crops can be grown twice a year; the land is not arid and it is rare for people to go hungry, apart from in the drier areas such as Karamoja. The result is that if someone does not have employment he can usually go back to the village, plant some crops, and have enough to eat. This is different from Kenya, where there is not enough fertile land, and if Kenyans don't have a job they will starve. This difference has resulted in a more laid-back attitude to work in Ugandans. As a generalization, Ugandans will be more open and friendly than their Kenyan brothers, who appear more businesslike, but they may not have as strong a work ethic, since they will always have something to eat.

Increasing urbanization, with the migration of the unskilled rural poor to Kampala, has resulted in a high rate of unemployment, with many in urban slums eking out a living. There are also young Ugandan graduates who find it hard to get employment, often because they have trained in the wrong subjects or skill set. Such young people are increasingly open to developing entrepreneurial skills for job creation. The government, NGOs, and large businesses are beginning to realize that they need to facilitate appropriate vocational training and business incubation centers in order to take advantage of this ready pool of labor.

ATTITUDES TOWARD WEALTH
The attitude of Ugandans to wealth is ambiguous. There are many who despise the ill-gotten gains of the nouveau riche who cannot explain where their recent wealth has come from, except that they have certain political connections and are involved in deal-making. However, there are others who will not question the source of the wealth, as long as there is the chance they will benefit personally. Of late, there has been a swing of opinion against those who have amassed fortunes by dubious means, since

many ordinary people realize that such enrichment is ultimately at the expense of the country. The tide has not yet turned completely against the rich man of dubious reputation, but there are signs that it is turning.

As a generalization, in Africa a man is judged by how well he can provide for his family. Therefore if he has the opportunity to gain financially through his connections or his job, he may be seen as being irresponsible if he does not take it. Thus the virtue of being a good provider for one's family is weighed against one's responsibility toward an employer who may well be regarded as having a broad back—such as the government. There is a well-known saying that one eats where one works, meaning that the work may not provide a large salary but it does provide the opportunity for finding money by other means.

STATUS

As in other countries, there are many forms of status. For example, a family may have status by virtue of being related to the royal family of a tribe, and a person may have status by virtue of his position, being a senior civil servant or a senior medical consultant. A person who does not have such status may simply cultivate a successful image by driving a nice car, buying the drinks at the bar, and wearing an expensive suit. These symbols of outward success are considered important by many, who feel that if the image is cultivated first, success will follow.

THE AFRICAN "BIG MAN" SYNDROME

"Big men" (chiefs, kings, men of power)
have a unique position in African societies.
Much of what we experience in Uganda
today is because of this "big man"
mentality: there is a mindset that "big
men" must be pleased at all costs and that
ordinary laws don't strictly apply to them.
If someone is a president, a cabinet
minister, or a member of the government,
that person is deserving of special
treatment. There is ample room for cultural
misunderstanding here. In the West such
people are held to a higher standard of
accountability, and Western "big men"
have been forced to resign over mere
misdemeanors.

Take President Clinton as an example:
after the Monica Lewinsky incident he was
dragged before an impeachment hearing.
If he had been an African Big Man—in the
unlikely event that such behavior was made
public—the general reaction would have
been: What's all the fuss about? In Africa
we treat Big Men differently, and instead
of holding people in high places to higher
standards of behavior, they get special
exemptions. One can see this every day as
government-registered vehicles make
their own special lanes to by-pass the
lines of traffic.

ATTITUDES TOWARD OTHER TRIBES, THE REGION, AND FOREIGNERS

Ugandans are not tribalistic in the sense of having a deep-seated animosity to other tribes. They are proud of their own tribe, but have no motivation to go to war or persecute another tribe over tribal issues. On the other hand, there is always background talk about how one tribe is profiting most from the political administration, and it is common for squabbles to break out in the workplace over accusations of favoritism of one tribal group over another when someone is promoted. Politically this has already been alluded to under "Balancing the Cabinet" (see page 38).

The East Africa Community, which includes Uganda, Kenya, Rwanda, Burundi, and Tanzania, now has a Secretary General and a secretariat, and a number of regional barriers have been dismantled for the movement of goods and people. The region is likely to have monetary union within two years. Tanzania has exhibited signs of hesitation in the implementation of the Union, but Uganda has been going full steam ahead, even though it means that some of the top jobs are already going to Kenyans. Rather than being jealous, Ugandans have tended to criticize themselves and commend the Kenyans for being hard workers. Perhaps Ugandans appear to be passive in allowing Kenyans to take their jobs because they have a secret plan, since many Kenyan men who come to the country to work succumb to the charms of Ugandan women and become absorbed into Ugandan society!

As a rule, Ugandans are very tolerant of foreigners, though there is a gradation. They appear to have little or no problem with those from the region, and no issues with Europeans or Americans. They are still ambivalent toward Indians, despite the fact that Indians constitute the largest ethnic block doing business and providing jobs in Uganda. There is a saying that if you work for a white you will be used, but he will teach you, but if you work for an Indian you will just be used. The attitude to the Chinese is still evolving. Due to the language and cultural gap the Chinese have yet to show whether they will integrate with the population.

chapter three

CUSTOMS & TRADITIONS

FOLKLORE

Since Buganda is the largest kingdom, it accounts for much of the folklore of Uganda as a whole—which is not to say that the other kingdoms and regions don't have their own histories and folklore. The ancient oral history about the origins of Buganda is largely made up of myths, stories, and folklore, the most significant involving Kintu, the first Kabaka.

In Baganda tradition a Muganda (Baganda

individual) passes through the stages of *omwana* (child), *omuvubuka* (youth), and *omusajja* or *omukazi* (man or woman). At death he becomes an *omuzima* (spirit) and a candidate for reincarnation. There is no initiation from youth to manhood, as there is among the Bagishu in the east, where the rite of passage is circumcision, but a Muganda youth is

HOW DEATH CAME TO EARTH

The story goes that Kintu married Nambi, but Nambi had to return to heaven because her father, Gulu, objected to the marriage, as Kintu did not know how to farm. Kintu then had to undergo a test in order to determine his suitability as a spouse, and was asked to identify his own cow in a herd—a difficult task. But a bee whispered to Kintu that he should choose the cow on whose horns he would alight. Several large herds were brought, and the bee had not identified a cow, so Kintu reported that his cow was not among them. Eventually, however, the bee did land, and Kintu identified his cow, along with several calves that had been born to it. This amazed the father, who eagerly gave his daughter's hand in marriage.

Gulu then urged the couple to hurry and leave for Kintu's home as soon as possible before Walumbe, the Spirit of Death, came. They were warned that they should not turn back, even if they forgot something, but Nambi went back to collect some grain, and although she tried to run away from Walumbe, she did not succeed. Hence, after many years of happiness on Earth, Walumbe began to bring illness and death. Up to the present day, Death has lived upon the Earth, with no one knowing when or whom he will strike.

generally perceived to have become a man when he takes a wife.

There is also a tradition that at birth the umbilical cord is retained for later use in a ceremony called Kwalula Abaana. During this ceremony the child gathers with other members of the father's clan to receive the clan names. However, such a tradition is no longer widely practiced, although in the case of the Kabaka the umbilical cord is kept as a sacred object.

The Royal Umbilical Cord
When the King is born the umbilical cord is kept by a minister, who has the title of Keeper of the Royal Umbilical Cord. It is wrapped in the traditional Baganda cloth made from the bark of the *mutuba* tree, and as the years go by more layers are added, so that the bundle gradually assumes the shape of a human being. The tradition is related to keeping connection with the ancestors.

Bark Cloth
The process of making bark cloth (*olubugo*) is called *okukomagga*, and the Kkobe clan is traditionally responsible for preparing the king's coronation bark cloth dress. Tradition has it that bark cloth was discovered during the generation of Kabaka Kintu, the first King of Buganda, which explains why Buganda as a society was more advanced than surrounding tribes.

The inner bark of the *mutuba* tree *(Ficus natalensis)* is harvested during the wet season and then beaten with different types of wooden mallets to make its texture soft and give it an even terracotta color. It is traditionally used for clothing, bedding, and shrouds. It is also a respected item in burial and other cultural ceremonies of communities other than the Baganda. *Engabo* (kings' guards) in the Toro kingdom are identified by their bark cloth uniforms, and in the Bunyoro kingdom bark cloth is used in their cultural ceremonies. The *olubugo* can also be used as an alternative to canvas by painters, due to its varying textures and durability.

Both men and women wear bark cloth like a toga, women tying a sash around the waist. It is worn mainly at coronations and healing ceremonies, funerals, and cultural gatherings. The

production of bark cloth prospered with workshops in almost every village in the Buganda kingdom until the abolition of cultural institutions in Uganda under the Obote regime after independence.

Night Dancers

There is a myth or belief that some Ugandans have the ability to transform themselves into night dancers. These are beings that appear only at night, sometimes floating above the ground; they are naked and can raise cadavers so that they can be transported to their home where they will be dismembered and eaten by the night dancers. If a living person has the misfortune to meet a night dancer he may also be slain and eaten. While the roots of this belief are in the Kiganda religion, some disturbed people believe in it to the extent that they roam around naked at night terrorizing the community. Night dancing is regarded as a recognized condition, akin to some kind of mental illness, or being "possessed" by spirits.

PUBLIC HOLIDAYS

The main public holidays in Uganda mirror those in Western societies, that is, Christmas, New Year's Day, Easter, and Labor Day. Added to these are the Eid Muslim holidays, Independence Day, Heroes' Day, NRM Liberation Day, and Martyrs' Day.

Martyrs' Day commemorates the persecution and martyrdom between the years 1885 and 1889 of at least forty-five Christian converts by Kabaka Mwanga II. At the time Kabaka Mwanga was in a precarious situation, with his authority being undermined by Christian and Muslim missionaries. Those of his subjects who had converted to Christianity renounced the traditional rites of the Kiganda religion, plus his own homosexual practices (thought to have been introduced by the Arab traders from Zanzibar). This action was an affront to an absolute monarch, and the baptized page boys were executed (see page 56). They were both Catholic and Protestant, and twenty-two of the Catholic martyrs were canonized as saints during the visit of Pope Paul VI to Uganda in 1964.

CALENDAR OF PUBLIC HOLIDAYS

New Year's Day	January 1
NRM Liberation Day	January 26
International Women's Day	March 8
Good Friday	Movable
Easter Monday	Movable
Labor Day	May 1
Uganda Martyr's Day	June 3
Heroes' Day	June 9
Independence Day	October 9
Christmas Day	December 25
Boxing Day	December 26

Eid-ul-Fitr (end of Ramadan) and **Eid-ul-Adha** (Feast of Sacrifices) are also public holidays. The dates are variable and are determined by the Saudi Muslim calendar.

GREETINGS

Greetings in Uganda can be confusing to the average Westerner used to simple one-word greetings such as "Hi" and "'Bye," but foreigners need not become overly anxious since they are given a great deal of latitude. Traditionally, greetings are long and unhurried. One asks not only how the night was, and after the health of the person and their family, but also after their household, including their animals. These long greetings are interspersed with pauses and many drawn out "ehs" as one thinks of the next thing to say. It is also polite in most tribes to thank the person: the thanks can be indiscriminate, and in English it may sound odd when someone thanks you for "whatever you are doing," but that is the direct translation. It is safer to greet in English, when one can just say "How are you?" to which most people will respond "I'm fine" or "Fine, how are you?" Children will call after whites, "*Mzungu*, how are you?" since this is what they have picked up from school. The word *mzungu* literally means "white man running around," and was coined when white people first came to Uganda because they seemed to be so restless. Some whites don't like to be addressed like this, but it is not meant with any ill intent and it is better to respond, "Fine, how are you?" or even "*Jendi*," which means "Fine."

The morning greeting in Luganda is, "*Wasuze otya no?*" which literally means, "How was your night, my dear?" But by ten in the morning you can change that greeting to "*Osibye otya no?*" which means, "How is your day, my dear?" You can then thank the person for his work (this is simply being polite and expressing general appreciation for the work that you presume the person has carried out, or he may be digging in the garden, for which you are giving more specific appreciation), you can give them peace, you can ask after the family, and so on. These elaborate greetings are mainly carried out in the vernacular. If an elder is greeting a child or a young woman in the vernacular, the young person will slip on to their knees as they respond. This is a sign of respect for elders and does not indicate subservience of females, but good manners, and that the person has been well brought up. Even educated professional women will greet their elders while kneeling if they are in a traditional context. In a good home, with well brought up children, the girls kneel to greet their parents even if they are "modern" women.

One can shake hands with both men and women, and there are no taboos about touching except in the case of one's mother-in-law, who must not be touched, and some Muslim sects.

BAPTISMS AND CHRISTENINGS

When a baby is born it is normal to have it baptized, in both in the Anglican and Roman Catholic traditions. Among the more affluent there will be a church service followed by a reception and a meal, while in the village a number of babies may be baptized together after the normal Sunday service.

Two for the Price of One

While I was working in a remote rural area, the local Anglican pastor was part of our immunization team, and would carry out mass baptism after the babies had been vaccinated. It seemed like an efficient use of resources.

MARRIAGE PRACTICES

Marriage practices have been influenced by tradition. Ugandan society was traditionally polygamous—a man had several wives, each installed in a separate hut in his compound. This is still the practice in South Sudan, where, although the South Sudanese are strongly Christian, they are officially polygamous. Over the past generation polygamy in Uganda, apart from within the Muslim community, has been officially dropped, and formal marriage is to one wife. However, despite this, informal polygamy has continued.

A woman is recognized as formally married only when the husband has paid the bride price, which may be several cattle or an agreed sum of money. Although this custom is dying out among the more educated, it is still common in rural areas. Thus a man may visit the parents to agree a bride price and obtain permission; however, many men then fail to complete payment of the full bride price and the marriage is never formalized. The result is that if the man does not provide adequately for his wife she is free to move on. On the other hand, if the bride price has been fully paid and she wishes to split from her husband, she will be advised to stay with the husband, since she is now his "property."

The term "husband" is used whether or not a bride price has been paid, and can be translated loosely as "my man," but in many cases the relationship is temporary. Young couples in a steady relationship who visit Uganda will find it easier to introduce their partner simply as their husband or wife. Young Ugandans have witnessed the traditional polygamous practices of their parents' generation. Indeed, it is not unusual for siblings to discover half-brothers and -sisters at the funeral of their father, who had another family, when the first family was unaware of the existence of the other. Such situations understandably give rise to property disputes, particularly where the man died intestate. Recently the Ugandan parliament sought to introduce a marriage and divorce bill to bring marriage practices up to date, but was forced to drop it because there was so much disagreement on the definition of marriage itself.

Weddings

Ugandans generally have two wedding ceremonies. First is the *kwanjula* or *kohinjira* (the names given to the traditional ceremony in the central area and the western region respectively), in which the bride and groom are introduced, the bride price is settled, and gifts are exchanged. This traditional wedding used to suffice, but now, after the advent of

Christianity and Islam, a church wedding, civil ceremony, or Islamic wedding is added, with the date for this set at the first ceremony.

Some traditional weddings were simply a delegation of men coming from the neighboring hill or village to negotiate with the family over a certain woman. When negotiations were complete, the group would carry off their prize and that was that. Traditions have more or less been modified, or modernized, and some of the *kwanjulas* are highly stylized, with professional negotiators, and the bride hidden among many sisters and aunts, Old Testament-style. However, the negotiations are generally good humored, and the bride is presented as one of many beautiful African maidens, attired demurely in colorful traditional dress. Often she does not get to play much of a role in the whole ceremony, simply being presented to her future husband at the beginning and then being chased back into hiding for the remainder.

Sealing the Deal

Occasionally the negotiations can take a serious turn: I was present at one *kwanjula* in which the family of the groom were strict evangelical Christians who would not touch alcohol, but the family of the bride insisted that the negotiations be concluded in the traditional way, with a calabash of beer sealing the deal. The impasse was broken by the negotiator who sneaked in the beer to satisfy the traditional in-laws.

In another case, this time in a Karamajong traditional ceremony where the girl was marrying an expatriate, the elders put a very high price on the bride, in the form of a number of cattle. The bridegroom did not have enough money to purchase the animals, so they reluctantly accepted a payment plan.

The church wedding, followed by a reception, can take the form of a huge gathering. These have become more and more elaborate over time and enormously expensive, emulating weddings in

Western countries but on an even grander scale. A modest wedding reception can accommodate three or four hundred people, while it is not uncommon to have a reception for a thousand guests. The funds for such an event are raised though wedding meetings, in which a committee is formed to organize the event, and friends pledge money to cover various expenses. One sometimes wonders if this is the best use of time and money, but it has become a modern tradition to make each reception big, brash, and expensive. If the couple happens to have a rich father who wants to impress his friends with his success, then the lavishness of the wedding and the reception may know no bounds.

The *Ssenga*

Perhaps the history of polygamy explains the attitude of the Ugandan woman toward her man. In the West, once the couple is married the responsibility is on both parties to stay faithful, and if the man strays there is immediate justification for the woman to launch divorce proceedings and relieve him of half of his worldly possessions. In Uganda, when a woman is being prepared for marriage she will have a meeting with the *ssenga*, the sister of her father. This aunt has the task of preparing the young bride for marriage, and the practice has continued both in rural and in urban areas, in poor and in rich families.

The general theme is on how to please your man, and on how to deal with any tendency toward philandering. The psychology is that he will inevitably stray, but it's the wife's duty to be as delectable as possible so that she minimizes the risk. In the event, she must also learn how to bring him back into the fold. To this end various herbs and rituals have traditionally been used, and advice given on how to keep the man so sexually satisfied that he does not want to leave the house. Beads are often worn around the waist, which is thought to have a certain sexual potency, and in the central region girls have traditionally been encouraged to "pull" their labia in order to elongate them—thought to be attractive to the man in that they wrap around his manhood and so give him more sensation. Most modern girls have rebelled against this painful tradition. The practice is not to be confused with female genital mutilation, which has never been widespread in Uganda, although it is traditionally carried out in some areas (see page 84).

Traditionally the *ssenga* would accompany the young couple into the bedroom on their bridal night to ensure that everything went smoothly; then, if the event was crowned with success, she would emerge from the bedroom with the proof of the bride's maidenhead having been broken, resulting in a goat being slain and a village celebration. However, it is some time since such customs have been strictly observed.

FUNERALS

When a person dies, it is normal not only for the family and close friends to attend the funeral, but also friends of friends, and friends of relatives, and those who attend because the deceased was a well-known person.

A Christian funeral involves a vigil at the home, a church service, and the burial, which will usually be in the ancestral village. It usually lasts late into the evening, or all night, and many people sleep over. It is literally a matter of sitting with the relatives to show solidarity. The church service will take place the day after the vigil, followed by the burial at the village home. It is very unusual for people to be buried in a public cemetery or a church graveyard as known in the West.

A Compelling Excuse

It is very common for staff to be away from work because they have had to attend a funeral. This is regarded as a legitimate reason for absence, particularly if one works in a government department. When the boss hears that a staff member has gone to the funeral of his mother he is sympathetic, but if the same person then takes time off again for another funeral of his mother, he may become suspicious. The explanation given is that the first funeral was for his real mother, while the second was for his aunt, but in local tradition it is respectful to refer to the sister of your mother also as your mother. This explanation is likely to be understood and, in most cases, considered acceptable by the boss—unless he is particularly tough.

Last Funeral Rites

A few weeks, or even a year, after the funeral there will be "the last funeral rites." This is a ceremony in which the responsibilities of the deceased person are passed on to another family member. If it was a mother who died, the responsibility for her children might be passed on to her sister. If she had made a will, she would have named the person to take over her responsibilities, but in the absence of a will the elders of the clan decide. The custom predates Christianity in Uganda and stems from the traditional religion, but has to a large extent been absorbed into the various prevailing religions, so that there is often singing of hymns, prayers, and little to do with any Kiganda ritual. Today, in a more materialistic society, who is named as the heir or successor is also important since there may be financial implications.

Funeral rites usually involve staying the night at the ancestral home. Many of these ceremonies take place in the village and the local people build temporary tent-like shelters of banana leaves. Since this provides an opportunity for men and women to get together in intimate circumstances, many children have been begotten at these funeral rites gatherings— completing the cycle of life.

WITCHCRAFT

As we have seen, traditional pre-Christian Kiganda religion had one supreme deity, Katanga, and a number of other semi-deities and lower spirits who could be invoked or appeased through various rituals and forms of sacrifice. There are several well-known shrines in Uganda, and many lesser clan and family shrines, where people go to perform rituals or make sacrifices in order to obtain the blessing of the spirits and good fortune in their lives. Witch doctors, or shamans, are the keepers of these shrines, and are regarded as having special magical powers. Sometimes "witchcraft" is associated with the practice of herbal medicine, but traditional healers are, at least in theory, in a different category from sorcerers who use rituals, incantations, and sacrifice. A recent survey showed that at least 20 percent of Ugandans admitted to believing in witchcraft, though the definition of witchcraft is not clear cut. Some consider anyone involved in keeping the shrines and all traditional healers as witch doctors, so the boundaries are blurred. With many people being highly superstitious, there is no shortage of believers in what some refer to as traditional religion and others call witchcraft.

In Uganda, traditional cultures sit side-by-side with modern practices. Although some ancient customs have died out, traditions still have a strong hold on society, and one should bear in mind that animism is a part of Africa's roots and culture. Whether or not one agrees with such beliefs, it is best to recognize that under the surface they still exert an influence on how people think. It is not uncommon for businessmen to fall back on traditional Kiganda beliefs, rituals, and sacrifices in the hope of bringing good fortune to their enterprises.

Women sometimes wear a string of beads around their waists as a charm to encourage fertility. Mothers will also have their baby's ear pierced for the very practical reason of protecting the child against kidnapping and child sacrifice. A child will not be kidnapped if he is considered to be blemished in any way.

HERBAL MEDICINE

Herbal medicine is widely available in Uganda, and many patients seek such treatment first, before attending the hospital or clinic. There are, in fact, many medicinal plants and proven remedies for conditions such as heart failure (*Digitalis*) and malaria (*Artemether*). While some research is being carried out on testing and quantifying these traditional remedies, there is still much work to be done in this field.

FEMALE GENITAL MUTILATION, AND CIRCUMCISION

The practice of Female Genital Mutilation (FGM) takes place in Uganda, particularly among the Sabene tribe on the Kenyan border. As some NGOs and government agencies have tried to educate the population against the practice, it has tended to move underground and be carried out secretly.

Male circumcision is practiced by Muslims, and is also a rite of passage to manhood among the Bagishu tribe in the east of Uganda. In this region every male who has reached puberty should submit himself for circumcision, which is performed on alternate years. If anyone does not submit himself, groups of men in traditional dress, painted white, will seek out the non-

circumcised and carry out the procedure forcefully, without anesthetic. Although the ritual still takes place, there are a number of Bagishu men who are now not so keen on the tradition and have been known to flee the area when circumcision frenzy is in the air.

As it happens, all adult males are now being encouraged by the government and the World Health Organization to undergo circumcision as a measure to reduce the transmission of HIV. While circumcision does not prevent the transmission of HIV, it has been shown to reduce transmission from female to male by 60 percent. Therefore although from an individual point of view there is no guarantee that the procedur will prevent the transmission of HIV, from a public health point of view it is a worthwhile exercise. This circumcision is usually carried out by nurses, who use local anesthetic.

chapter four

MAKING FRIENDS

FRIENDSHIP BETWEEN UGANDANS

As in many societies that are not very physically mobile, Ugandans tend to mix with the people they grew up with or went to school with. It is common to discover that people are old school buddies, or that they are related, or their cousin is married to her sister, and so on. In other words, it is not very difficult to find a connection between Ugandans.

Family is very important, and people tend to put loyalty first to family, then to friends,

then to the organization they work for.
In times of need friends will rally round,
depending on the degree of closeness, but
when it comes to financial obligations people
will generally turn to someone they are
related to. Where a friendship has been close
since childhood, the friend will be considered
a member of the family even if he is not a
blood relative, and be referred to by the
children as "Uncle."

It is common to express one's care for
another person tangibly, through the giving
of gifts and providing for their needs. Helping
out is a mark of friendship. This is not to
suggest that friendship should be based on
money, but you should not become offended
if a Ugandan friend asks for help in some
way. This situation is more likely to arise in a
village context than in an urban setting where
people are better off.

SOCIALIZING

The easiest place to meet Ugandans is at
work, and some expatriates who work in
embassies or aid agencies where they do
not meet many Ugandans have difficulty
breaking into Ugandan social circles. One can
meet people with common interests at clubs
such as the "Jam Session" at the National
Theatre, the "Hash" (a regular Monday night
jogging club followed by dinner and drinks),
and various cultural societies such as the
French or German societies and the Rotary

Club, which is very popular. There are also business gatherings and sports clubs. If you are working in a rural area, the best way to get to know people is to visit them in their homes, especially in the evenings when they are preparing food and one can sit outside and chat as the food is cooking. One can also meet people in bars and nightclubs, though one should choose with care if one wishes to avoid commercial sex workers.

As a generalization, Ugandans are friendly and hospitable to outsiders, though they will not go out of their way to invite them to functions such as dinner parties at home, or even to return such hospitality. To an English person, who is used to a certain degree of formal reciprocity, this may be off-putting, but if you care to invite yourself to a Ugandan's home, or express interest in attending family functions such as weddings, funeral rites, or baptisms, then you will be made most welcome.

Ugandans tend to socialize in small pubs, or perhaps under a tree where a group will gather informally, and not necessarily in one another's homes. Different pubs, shops, clubs, and restaurants become associated with various groups of people. For example, the Kampala Club or the Golf Club are regular hangouts for ministers and government officials, so one can go there to meet the movers and shakers. On the other hand, one might find a group of generals at a particular small *kafunda* (bar) on the street. Certain bars are well known for the younger crowd, such as the Steak Out, and expatriates also tend to gravitate to bars such as the Irish Pub, where there is a mixed group of Ugandans and non-Ugandans. Some meeting places are well known for "ladies of the night," while other clubs pride themselves on being entirely free from this type of clientele. Ugandan society is not very stratified, either by age or social standing, so both men and women can hang out in most places, no matter what age or color, without any taboos or anyone taking much notice.

TRANSACTIONAL SEX

Since there are many commercial sex workers, particularly in the urban areas, a significant number of non-Ugandans (as well as many thousands of Ugandans) have contracted HIV. The sex trade in Uganda is not as clearly defined as in some other countries, where the transaction is negotiated first so that everyone knows where they stand. Many of the young women in the bars will simply befriend a stranger and not ask him for money. If one picks up a hooker on the street it is easy to define the transaction, but if one meets a beautiful girl in a bar who doesn't ask for anything except a drink, it is more difficult to define who she is. In fact, these girls are often more interested in a gentleman's possessions than in sex, and many a man wakes up in the morning to find that the girl has vanished along with all his worldly goods. If one is going to go to bars late at night, there are several rules that should be followed: preferably go with a crowd, don't go alone since you are then the proverbial sitting duck; take the money you need, and no more, since in the morning your balance will automatically be zero. Have a cab driver organized; leave your valuables, including your cell phone, behind. If you need to be contacted, take a cheap cell phone and not your prized new one with all your contacts and information. Girls should always go with a friend and never allow themselves to be lured into dark corners or lonely places—even if a bag is snatched it is not wise to pursue the thief, as it may be a trap. There are some pubs and clubs where there are no prostitutes, while there are others that are well known for that type of clientele, and others that have a mixture. It is easy to ask around and find out which is which.

There is a perception, sometimes encountered by mixed-race couples, that if a Ugandan woman is with a white guy she is there to extract all she can from him, and, moreover, this is regarded as legitimate, since why else would she be with a weak white guy except for his money?

LENDING MONEY

As we have seen, it is not uncommon for people to borrow money from their friends, though some Ugandans have turned this into a loan-sharking business. It is the norm for Ugandan families to be under pressure from relatives who are looking for handouts in the form of school fees, getting them jobs, or just giving them food or money, so it is not just the visiting *mzungu* who is targeted. One should also realize that the definition of "borrowing" in Uganda is not exactly as in the dictionary. If someone "borrows" some money, you should expect it to be a very elastic arrangement, and perhaps you should consider it simply as a gift. This is not to say that you will not be paid back, but it would be better to give the money (or decline to give it), rather than lend it and then be offended or hurt if your friend does not pay you back; the definition of "borrowing" and "giving" can easily get lost in translation. It also makes life simpler.

MIXED-RACE RELATIONSHIPS

Ugandans are not very judgmental, so they will usually not disapprove of a mixed-race relationship. However, good families do prefer their children to marry into a good Ugandan family and, given the choice, they would prefer their child to marry one of their own. On the other hand, like most parents, they simply want their children to be happy and well provided for, so the choice is left to the individual. There are many mixed marriages that are successful, and like all relationships there are some that don't work.

It is not uncommon for middle-aged foreign men, perhaps struggling with their marriage at home, to come to Uganda and be seduced by the friendly, accommodating women they meet in a bar, and abandon their wife back home. This is probably not the best basis to start a relationship, and many such relationships don't last the course. Some white men have a problem when it comes to meeting the right type of girls, because most educated Ugandan girls don't go out of their way to pick up a white man. White girls for some reason seem to gravitate toward Ugandan guys with dreadlocks. This may be because they seem more laid back, or less threatening, than the average Ugandan male— or perhaps they just like dreads.

CONVERSATION

When one joins a gathering, particularly where there are older members present, it is polite to go around the room, greet, and shake hands with everyone. This is not necessary in informal settings, such as pubs, though it is a good way to get to know people. In many gatherings people will be quite formal and may take several hours to relax—under the influence of some spirit—so the "after party" is where the party is more likely to take off.

In Uganda there are certain subjects and words that should not be used in conversation since they are considered rude, for example naming the genitals or sexual acts. Ugandans generally avoid the specifics, in the same way as we do when talking about "sleeping with" someone when referring to having sex. The majority of Ugandans are also somewhat sensitive about gay and lesbian relationships, and it is best to give the topic a wide berth.

All Ugandan men support an English Premier League soccer team, and it is a safe way to strike up a conversation, though the women will greet football with one big yawn. Politics is discussed *ad nauseam*, but it is difficult for the visitor to enter fully into the discussion since he is unlikely to be familiar with the local scene.

INVITATIONS

Formal invitations to someone's home will occur in the case of special celebrations, such as the baptism of a new baby, a birthday party, or *kwanjula*. One occasion where the dress code is formal is the *kwanjula*, where the members of

the groom's party are expected to wear
traditional dress. In the case of Buganda
Kingdom, the women wear the *gomeza* (a
traditional dress introduced in the nineteenth
century by the missionaries) while the men
wear the *kanzu* (a long, simple, shirt-like cotton
garment worn with suit trousers and jacket).
One must turn up on time for a *kwanjula*,
but other events tend to run late, and many
Ugandans appear to have adopted the habit of
arriving fashionably late. However, they apply
different standards to *mzungus* (whites), who
are known to be punctual.

Food at functions is usually served buffet-
style, and one may or may not be given a fork,
since it is normal to eat with the fingers. Hand-
washing facilities are provided at the beginning
of the line, usually by someone pouring water

from a jug. After the meal water is again provided to wash the hands. Food is not eaten from communal plates as in Ethiopia or Sudan. It is important that one stays until food has been served and consumed, and if one does arrive late it is preferable to arrive before the food has been served. When leaving a function it is good manners to greet the host and inform him that you must leave.

chapter five

UGANDANS AT HOME

HOUSING

The typical house in a Ugandan village is made of mud and wattle, with a skeleton of interwoven sticks and the spaces between filled in with mud. In the past the roofs were made of thatch, but increasingly the thatch has been replaced with corrugated iron sheets.

The next step up from the mud and wattle house with a corrugated iron roof is a brick and cement house with a roof of corrugated iron sheets. The bricks are made from locally available clay, which is dug out of the ground, mixed with

water, and shaped into bricks using wooden molds. These bricks are first dried in the sun and then built into a structure in the shape of a kiln, which is fired by placing wood inside it for at least twenty-four hours. The results are fired handmade bricks that are always slightly different sizes, since the molds are not standardized. When the bricks have cooled, the kiln is disassembled brick by brick, and the bricks used for building.

Priorities

When I first lived in Luwero, in Uganda, twenty-seven years ago, just after the end of the bush war, most people lived in a thatched mud hut and slept on a mat on the floor. As they gained a little disposable income, they invested in three essentials. The first was a foam mattress, the second was a bicycle, and the third was iron sheeting for the roof of their house.

In the village there are not many walls around individual houses, with people's houses and compounds being open, and one being free to wander from house to house. The compound may be the piece of land accommodating a single house, or a larger area with several houses belonging to members of the same family. The surface of the compound may have grass, or simply baked earth that is swept carefully every day.

In the city, up to the time of Idi Amin, security was not an issue, and houses were not hidden behind high walls and barred windows. In pre-colonial and the immediate post-colonial times there was very little in the way of thieving or housebreaking, because there was a general orderliness. During the Amin era, he would hang thieves next to the Clock Tower, a well-known landmark, in public executions—a discouragement to the thieving fraternity. After Amin, people started to build homes like fortresses, with security gates, barred windows, and high walls around their compounds. The result of this was that families became more isolated, living behind high walls, and behaving like Western families who don't know their neighbors.

As we have seen, today, even though Ugandans living in the city are still very hospitable, it is more common to meet them at social functions, bars, churches, or pubs, than to be invited back to their homes. Perhaps this is also due to the changing nature of family life, in which the home is organized around the well-defined needs of the nuclear family. It is bad manners for Ugandans not to welcome visitors and insist that they stay for food, so the previous practice was to make more food than the family needed, just in case someone came calling, but in the modern world this is just not practical anymore.

Home from Home

In Ireland the same thing used to happen. My mother would say, "Put another potato in the pot"—the potato was our staple food— and if someone called we would say, "Would you not take a wee bite to eat?"

Unlike in South Africa, where one still finds African townships with uniformly poor housing and extreme poverty, Ugandan society is relatively integrated, in the sense that there has never been any planned segregation of rich and poor. In fact there is not much planning, so rich and poor live side by side by default. It is not uncommon to find a huge, ostentatious house and several mud huts right next door to each other in the city, while in the village the successful "big man" may build his enormous garish villa on the hill. It may be the only such house in the midst of homes with mud walls and tin roofs, but it is there to prove that the son of the village has made good. In some cases there is resentment of such obvious displays of wealth, but in most cases there is admiration, albeit in the hope that some of the wealth will be shared around.

The past twenty years have seen the emergence of a Ugandan middle-income group, which had been held back during the preceding wars and periods of insecurity. During those times inflation had been so bad that one could work for a whole month for the price of a bunch of *matoke* (a large stem of savory bananas used for cooking). Everyone had to hustle for a living and get by as best they could. Some of these middle-income earners are now home-owners, and Western architectural styles have gained ground among the Ugandan middle class.

Young people find it difficult to get enough money together to buy a home, so many of them rent apartments. Mortgages are available, but interest rates are high, and one must put down at least a 20 percent deposit. However, many young people start by buying a piece of land in the hope that one day they will be able to build a house on it for themselves or their parents. There is something in the psyche of Ugandans that drives them to own land, no matter how small the plot or how remotely located.

Twenty years ago it was uncommon for middle-income earners to own a vehicle; now it is the rule. This is to some extent a reflection of rising levels of income. One of the side effects of this is that the streets of Kampala are increasingly congested due to the exponential rise in vehicle ownership.

THE DEMOGRAPHIC BULGE

Uganda has a very small number of people working in the formal sector, and although there is a very large informal sector, it is difficult to measure. Therefore those who are captured by the tax net are a tiny fraction of the total population, mainly living in Kampala and other urban centers. The total number of people working in the public and the formal private sectors totals around one million—out of a population of thirty-four million. This means that those who have the means to develop a Western lifestyle represent a very small percentage of the population, and that most Ugandans are still in the categories of urban poor, who depend on casual employment, or rural poor, who depend largely on subsistence agriculture.

Fifty percent of the population is under the age of fifteen, and this demographic bulge means that there is potentially a vast labor market to be tapped into. Unfortunately the education and training system is not taking advantage of this, and there is high unemployment and underemployment among young people. Even so, there is also some highly professional young talent emerging.

Brain Drain

My own experience as a doctor is that Ugandan medics are among the best in the world. The only problem is that they are usually not in Uganda. The challenge is to provide the facilities and the working environment that will entice them to stay; otherwise Uganda and other African countries will continue to train doctors for the rest of the world.

WHO EARNS WHAT?

Like all African countries there are extremes, with some very rich people and many very poor. Life for those in the middle with decent jobs is not too hard, but life for the urban poor without jobs can be one continuous hustle. Life for the village peasant usually starts with a visit to the *shamba* (the plot where the crops are planted). This is done in the early morning before the sun gets hot. After working in the *shamba,* there is food to prepare and cook and other chores to do around the compound. Life in the village is simple and slow; people work, but not too hard, and there is always time to stop and chat with a neighbor, or rise from whatever one is doing to gaze at a passing car, or a stranger walking along the road.

In the city, if a person earns around a thousand US dollars a month (equivalent in Uganda shillings to 2,500,000 at current exchange rates) he can live comfortably and have a Western lifestyle. Of course the income necessary rises steeply if there is a family to support, school fees to find, or a mortgage to repay.

Quality of Life

I have had discussions with Ugandan returnees
who have told me that even though they earn less
in absolute terms than they would in London or
the USA, they have a better lifestyle in Uganda.
Although certain consumer goods are cheaper
and more readily available in developed countries,
there is little to beat the weather, friends, and
family at home.

The new graduate who works in an office may
start in an entry-level position earning 300,000
shillings (a little over US $100 per month).
Salaries in the formal sector then rise according
to seniority, with a junior manager earning one
to two million shillings, a middle-level manager
earning three to five million, and a senior
manager earning five to ten million. Of course
there are wide variations, with civil servants
generally earning considerably less. However, they
have other perks, and there are some government
organizations, such as the Uganda Revenue
Authority, or Kampala Capital City Authority,
which pay very well. Nurses, as in most countries,
are relatively poorly paid, while doctors are
reasonably well paid, with specialists being able
to command high fees. Certain skills, such as IT,
are in demand, and those who are skilled in
these areas can command a high salary.

Those who earn a few hundred thousand
shillings per month (one to two hundred US
dollars) can live on these salaries, but do not
have a Western lifestyle, that is, shopping at the
supermarket for Western foods, calling into the

pub on the way home from work for a beer, taking the children out for an ice-cream, or living in a smart apartment. Their salary, if properly budgeted, will buy local food, pay school fees at a local school, and pay rent in a less desirable part of town. Those who earn salaries of one to two hundred US dollars per month are normally drivers, tradesmen, or lower-level office workers.

At the other end of the spectrum are those who are fabulously wealthy. These also fall into two categories. There are those who have started businesses and made money legitimately. These could be in steel, transport, property, banking, or telecoms, and many of these successful entrepreneurs, though by no means all, are Ugandan Indians. There are also those who have made money in the professions, such as law or medicine. The other category of people who have made money are those who have been able to use their connections, either politically or through working in the public sector, to leverage contracts and make corrupt deals. It is difficult to see how a mid-level civil servant can suddenly have enough money to buy an expensive property, or own a string of businesses, when one computes his earnings from government salaries, but many such properties and businesses can be traced back to mid-level or senior civil servants. Such people collude with corrupt private-sector operators, inflate the prices, and share the spoils.

A SENSE OF STYLE
As a rule, Ugandans are very neat and well dressed, and the style of long hair sported by African-

Americans is generally not favored. This means that the vast majority of Ugandan men have short hair, neatly trimmed, and many have shaven heads. As the world has noted through observing President Obama turning gray during his term of office, African hair goes gray relatively early, usually starting in middle age. The funny thing is that it is relatively rare to see gray hair in Ugandan men, even those in their sixties and seventies. This is because most older men dye their hair without any feeling that it is a sign of vanity. Hair salons are ubiquitous, because there is always business: the men get their hair cut regularly and the older guys get it dyed, while the women do all sorts of amazing and wonderful things to their hair in terms of extensions, weaves, wigs, hairpieces, and straightening techniques, including the use of chemicals, tongs, and rollers.

White people often make the assumption that African hair is basically short and curly and fail to appreciate its potential and versatility. If a Ugandan girl lets her hair grow and has it relaxed, it will reach to the shoulders. The style she goes for is a matter of personal choice. Some opt for extensions, others for relaxers, cornrows, wigs, or weaves. Depending on the length and thickness of the extensions, the plaiting can mean spending twelve hours at the hairdresser. The upside is that the

workmanship need not be repeated for at least three months. In a weave the natural hair is first washed and plaited into cornrows, then the weave is sewn in. Of course there are those who choose the Afro style, but in Uganda this is also kept neat and relatively short. This has become known as the "Janet style" since it was popularized by Uganda's First Lady, Janet Museveni.

THE DAILY ROUND

In the village the day usually takes on a fairly simple routine. Breakfast may be some food left over from the previous day, such as cassava or *matoke*, and if the family is poor there may be no breakfast at all, with the children often setting off early to walk to school. Normally the mother goes off to dig the *shamba*, before the sun gets too hot. If there is a baby she will carry it on her back, but will put it down while she digs. By late morning she will return and do chores around the compound, such as drying the kidney beans or the coffee beans, or sorting grit from the rice. The man of the house may have some casual labor, in which case he will often go to work on his bicycle. If he has no formal work, he may help in the *shamba*, though in certain tribes, such as the Bakiga, he is not expected to work in the *shamba* and may just sit around and drink the local brew.

Boys and girls are brought up differently, with the girls being taught from an early age to do the chores around the house, cook, look after the other children, and fetch water and firewood. Boys are brought up with a sense of entitlement, and are generally not expected to do domestic work. In the rural areas where electrification is sparse, people will rise with the sun (usually around 6:30 a.m.). In the evenings they will bathe after dark, since they often bathe outside in the open; the evening meal will be eaten quite late, after which they will immediately go to bed. People will sit round and

chat as they wait for the meal to cook.

In urban areas, the typical day is probably very much like that of city dwellers in any other part of the world. The time the person sets out to work is governed by how far they have to travel and whether they have to travel across town, since the traffic in Kampala quickly becomes congested

during the rush hours. Many people don't eat breakfast and the office worker may catch a *matatu* (mini-bus taxi) or hail a *boda boda* (motorcycle taxi). The *boda bodas* will take one door-to-door and are very convenient, but are not the preferred means of daily transport, since they are relatively expensive and dangerous. Work generally starts at 8:00 a.m. and since many office workers have not taken breakfast, the first order of the day is to have a cup of tea.

Office work is similar to that in any Western country, with time taken up on meetings and e-mails, not to mention Facebook. In the evenings it is common for white-collar workers to stop off for a drink on the way home. Pubs that sell roast chicken or pork are particularly popular. The build-up of traffic can therefore spread throughout the evening, since while some people leave the office and travel home at 5:00 p.m., others may be travelling at any time up to 10:00 p.m. Those who have wives and families will usually eat at home, but those who are single will eat at the pub. Although salaries are not high in absolute terms, some people spend a surprising amount of time and money in the pub. However, toward the end of the month it will be noticeable that people are going home earlier as their bank account depletes.

Shopping is normally done in one of the numerous small supermarkets that have sprung up on every corner. Evening markets are also popular, and street vendors bring their wares right on to the sidewalks. It is common to see someone sitting beside several small piles of tomatoes or potatoes for sale. As one goes home in the evening

the streets are alive with all kinds of merchants
selling their wares—everything from airtime
cards to a complete evening dress.

There are a number of free TV channels, plus
a whole raft of digital channels (which are quite
expensive), so most middle-income earners will
own a TV. English Premier league football is
popular, but the best venue to watch matches is
in a sports bar. Pirated DVDs are available on
the latest movies for less than a dollar (US), so
watching DVDs is very popular.

GROWING UP IN UGANDA

Ugandans love children, but they are expected to
behave well, which in the words of the adage
means they should be "seen and not heard." All
Ugandan schools have uniforms and most insist
on short hair. Thus Ugandan parents find it
unusual that some international schools do not
prescribe either a uniform or a hairstyle, and

assume that the children attending such schools are ill disciplined. While some schools do not shy away from corporal punishment, the new generation of middle-class families is very indulgent with their children. Hence there are two different standards of parenting, with some following the Western model of children being given more leeway, while the traditional attitude to disciplining children can be quite harsh.

Children growing up in the village, or the slum, may be left largely to their own devices and will imbibe the attitudes of the society around them, while middle-class children will have a much higher degree of parental input. It is the norm for any parents who can afford the school fees (which in some cases are very modest) to send their children to boarding school at a young age, and thus leave discipline in the hands of the school.

In the extended family the whole family takes responsibility for the various children—who can be cousins, orphans, distant relatives, or just children who have been taken in. There may be absent fathers, or deceased biological parents, so aunts, uncles, grandparents, single mothers, all take responsibility. There is no "ideal" family, but Ugandan families demonstrate the greatest amount of flexibility when it comes to bringing up children.

EDUCATION

More than a decade ago the government
introduced UPE—Universal Primary Education.
This means, in theory, that there is free primary
education for all children, and the vast majority of
children attend school to at least twelve or thirteen
years old. Unfortunately, although the introduction
of free primary education was accompanied by an
increase in the education budget (supported by
donors), it was still insufficient, so there are very
large classes. The method of teaching is mainly by
rote, in the "repeat after me" style, so the students
therefore repeat the mistakes of their teachers.
The net result is that while there are many children
attending school, the actual standard of education
is relatively low. A recent survey carried out by the
World Bank found that many children who were
supposed to be at a fifth-grade level were in fact
performing at a second-grade level.

While primary education is compulsory, a
much smaller number of children go on to
secondary and tertiary education.

chapter six

TIME OUT

Ugandans are very gregarious—they like to socialize, drink, dance, and laugh. If there is pressure at work, they'll retire to the pub at the end of the day and have a drink and some *muchomo* (roast meat on a skewer), and the world will seem a better place.

In Uganda, personal relationships are important and may take priority over the task. This means that Ugandans will give time to the person first and allow other things to sort themselves out, so appointments may run behind time. When it comes to socializing and partying, the weekend gets extended.

Culture Shock

When some Ugandan friends of mine visited Rwanda they were looking for the social scene, which happens after work, so they were shocked that the city seemed dead on a weeknight. In Uganda there will always be something going on any night of the week. They say in Uganda that the weekend starts on Thursday and finishes on Monday, which means that the weekend has five days and the week has two.

NIGHTLIFE

There are several areas of Kampala that are well known for restaurants, bars, or nightclubs. Acacia Avenue near the Central Business District has a number of good restaurants, while Kisementi nearby has some well-known bars, good coffee shops, and bistros. The nightclubs are mainly to be found in the industrial area, with some outliers in Ntinda and Jinja Road, while Kabalagala, a suburb of Kampala, is studded with street bars, clubs, and pubs. If you are conscious of your budget you can frequent any number of small roadside joints that serve beer and *muchomo*. Areas such as Kabalagala continue until dawn, with roast chicken being sold by the side of the road for those who feel like a snack.

There are also a number of places that are more laid back. One wine shop and many of the small bars simply put chairs and tables in the car park with some music, and clients buy their drinks and sit and sip their wine or beer until the small hours of the morning—of course, buying more than the one bottle they had initially come for.

EATING OUT
Food

Uganda has a great variety of food. Its fertile agricultural land can grow practically anything. The Ugandans themselves favor plantains, particularly *matoke,* which is a green banana. *Matoke* is peeled when green, then mashed and steamed in the leaves, resulting in a yellowish, savory, mashed potato type of dish. It is a heavy food, with a high content of water that lies in the stomach and makes one feel sleepy; it is probably an acquired taste. Those who have grown up eating *matoke* are practically addicted to it, while those who are introduced to it in their adulthood can take it or leave it. Other common foods are beans and *posho* (maize flour that has been boiled into a thick, sticky porridge), groundnut sauce (peanut paste), spinach, avocados, tomatoes, meat, fish, and chicken.

The most common fish eaten in Uganda is tilapia, caught in Lake Victoria and several other lakes. It is a tasty freshwater fish, which is sometimes deep fried and served whole, or cooked with herbs in the oven. It is best eaten with the fingers, as are most Ugandan foods (Ugandans appear to have fingers made of

asbestos). Ugandan food is fresh, heavy, and sometimes spicy, but often plain.

Apart from Ugandan foods, there is a variety of international dishes available, including Indian, Thai, Chinese, Ethiopian, Japanese, and Middle-Eastern, served in a plethora of restaurants throughout Kampala and other Ugandan towns. Food can also be bought cooked at the roadside, or from markets and takeout vendors, of which there has been an upsurge in the past decade. The local chicken takeouts are particularly tasty. In the villages the diet is strictly traditional.

TIPPING

There is no set standard for tipping as there is in the USA, so you can tip according to the service, and a tip of 10 percent is considered generous. Many Ugandans do not tip at all, and generally foreigners are better tippers. Some restaurants add a service charge to the bill, but when you inquire from the staff, they often do not receive this (the restaurant claims it is for breakages). The bill may be inclusive of taxes, but some establishments add VAT (value added tax) and a local service tax to the prices stated in the menu, plus "service charge," so you may get a shock when the final bill is 23 percent greater than the menu prices.

Drinks

While Nairobi may be the recognized business capital of East Africa, Kampala is undoubtedly the social capital. This is due to several factors, not least among them being the enormous capacity of Ugandans to imbibe liquor, ranking first in East Africa and not far behind celebrated hard-drinking nations such as the Russians. In fairness to the Ugandans who frequent the pubs and clubs on Kampala's social scene, they are not the main culprits who drive up the statistics. This accolade goes to those who drink the local hooch, which includes *malwa* (local beer drunk from calabashes—large squashes—through long straws), and those who are brave enough to drink the locally distilled gin. The problem with the locally distilled stuff is that there is a risk of it being pure methanol, which makes people blind. One can depend on hearing of a number of cases of unfortunate people who succumb to this fate each year, so it is safer to stick to a known brand in a recognizable bottle.

The local branded gin is Uganda Waragi (UG). It is distilled safely by Ugandan Breweries and is

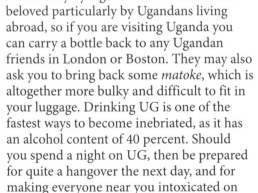

beloved particularly by Ugandans living abroad, so if you are visiting Uganda you can carry a bottle back to any Ugandan friends in London or Boston. They may also ask you to bring back some *matoke*, which is altogether more bulky and difficult to fit in your luggage. Drinking UG is one of the fastest ways to become inebriated, as it has an alcohol content of 40 percent. Should you spend a night on UG, then be prepared for quite a hangover the next day, and for making everyone near you intoxicated on the vapor that will hang on your breath for the next twenty-four hours.

For those who wish to stick to milder drinks, such as local beers, there are a number of good local beers that will quench your thirst and still allow you to function relatively soberly. One should, however, remember that the drunk-driving laws in Uganda have recently become strict, and a Ugandan police cell is not a tourist attraction one wants to experience firsthand, so it is wise to have a designated driver or to take a taxi home.

SERVICE

The level of service is variable. If you can afford to stay in the Serena Hotel, the foremost hotel in Kampala, the service will be excellent, while in some of the cheap local hotels it can be rather minimal. This is not to say that one only gets what one pays for and that service levels decrease unless you are paying through the nose. Obviously the more expensive hotels and restaurants have trained their staff well, not to mention that the customers tip more heavily, but Ugandans can give wonderful service if they are so inclined, since they are naturally empathetic. However, the pressures of life can also make them compartmentalize, so that while they are warm and friendly to family and friends they can be uninterested in a customer.

There is no reason to accept poor service anywhere, but sometimes all it takes is a smile to break the ice, and poor service may simply be due to problems of communication: the person may not answer you because she does not understand, not because she is being rude.

Much in Uganda functions on good relationships, and once you have made someone your friend, they will be very helpful. Ugandans themselves are now more demanding in terms of levels of service, and those who have returned from abroad are the most demanding.

SPORTS

Ugandans are football (soccer) crazy, at least the men are, and the women have no choice but to find something else to do or watch it with them. Playing football is the recreation of choice in Uganda, and a football is a great present for kids. The league of choice is the English Premier League and the favored teams are Arsenal, Chelsea, and Manchester United, though there are also a few Liverpool and Man City supporters. When there is a big match there will be a crowd of young men in the streets, watching the match through the open door of some bar.

These are the unfortunates who cannot even afford the price of a drink to gain admission. There are many popular sports bars with flat-screen TVs and projections on large screens where the crowds gather.

Uganda's national football team is known as the Cranes, named after the national bird. They are a talented team that has, on many occasions, snatched defeat out of the jaws of victory, usually falling at the last hurdle—failing in the qualifying rounds for the Africa Cup of Nations, or even the World Cup. However, this does not dampen the enthusiasm with which they will be followed in the next big match. More than any other sports team, the Cranes have the ability to unite Uganda. If there is a victory at the National Stadium, cars and *boda bodas* (motorcycle taxis) will be racing up and down the streets with horns blaring and flags flying. Even when one is at home, far away from the stadium, and the Cranes score, the roar can be heard throughout the whole of Kampala.

Uganda's greatest sportsman emerged as a surprise to most people. He is none other than the current Olympic marathon champion, Stephen Kiprotich. This small gentleman not only won the marathon at the London Olympics in 2012 but then went on to win the marathon at the World Championships in Russia the following year.

Other sports played in Uganda include cricket, golf

(there is a golf course in the middle of Kampala, one of the few remaining green areas), tennis, and rugby, which has built up a following among the middle-class corporate group.

A Moment to Savor

Being a bit of a jogger myself, I was seated in front of the TV to watch the entire Olympic marathon, not really in hope of a Ugandan triumph, but out of sheer admiration for the speed and endurance of the runners. Few Ugandans were even watching the race, as they had little hope that their man would be placed, since he was not seen as being among the favorites. For those who were watching, all eyes were on the Kenyans and the Ethiopians, and when the Kenyans made their final break, Kiprotich appeared to fall behind, so the cameras were not even covering him. Then he came out of nowhere on the bend and took over the race. It is so seldom that Ugandans witness such a victory that it is hard to describe the national pride that we all felt. It was an emotional moment.

THE ARTS
Music
There is a lively popular music scene in Uganda, with some long-established artists such as the Afrigo Band and Simba Sounds, and many new musicians who have taken the country by storm. Genres include pop, hip-hop, reggae, R&B, blues, gospel, jazz, South African, Congolese, folk, and fusion, among others. There are a number of music

awards, which seem to have spurred the development of new talent, and some local musicians have gone on to regional, Pan African, and even international acclaim.

Apart from the popular music scene there is some classical music, mainly from the Kampala School of Music, or the African International Music School. However, the opportunity for full symphony orchestra performances is limited, and if you like classical music you may have to make do with an occasional visiting string quartet.

Jazz has been promoted by one of the beer companies, such that there are regular jazz performances with well-known international artists performing.

On the local dance and drama front, there is the well-established Ndere Troupe, which performs traditional music and dance on a weekly basis at its venue in Kampala. There are also numerous cultural dance troupes, whose services are constantly in demand at functions and weddings. The traditional cultural instruments, including drums, render a melodious and interesting sound. They include the eight-stringed *enanga* or the nine-  stringed *adungu*, which is an arched harp; the *ndingidi*, which is a one-stringed fiddle; the *engalabi*, the long drum; the *ensosi*, shakers made from gourds; panpipes; the *amadinda*, the xylophone; and the thumb piano.

Jam Packed

Some years ago I used to attend "The Jam Session" on a regular basis. This was held in a small room at the National Theatre in Kampala. It was a jam session, both in the sense that people came and "jammed," and in the fact that we were literally jammed into the room. I often feared for what would happen if there were a fire, as there was only one exit. During that time, in the late '90s, Uganda was devastated by HIV, and many of the local artists died of AIDS. Every month there was the announcement of another death of someone we loved. The music scene was one of the sectors that was most devastated. One of Uganda's most popular musicians, Philly Lutaya, returned to Uganda to do a final concert to declare that he himself was infected, and to warn his fellow Ugandans about AIDS. He died soon afterward.

It was a staple at the jam session that someone would sing "No Woman No Cry." It was a kind of ritual, with no session being complete without a rendering. Sometimes the renderings were so bad and out of tune that I wanted to cry myself!

Dancing

While hymn singing will take place at funerals and funeral rites, drumming and dancing are common at all celebrations, including weddings, some church services, and other special occasions. Dancing in Uganda varies according to the origin of the dance and the tribe. Traditional Kiganda dancing from Buganda is very energetic, with particular emphasis on the movement of the feet, which results in vigorous shaking of the pelvis. Children learn to dance at school, and the average Westerner need not even try to imitate it, because he will dislocate something. Some of these dances have sexual connotations, having evolved to depict seduction, or the boy taking the girl off to his home, but others have different meanings, and many are designed in praise of the Kabaka (the king).

Dances are accompanied by drumming on variously sized drums, which are made of hollowed-out tree trunks over which goatskin is stretched and dried in the sun. Sometimes the drums are accompanied by other traditional stringed instruments, which sound somewhat like the ukulele. The music is lively and the dancing skilled. Kiganda dancing is from the central region of the country, but as one goes west the dancing becomes more muted and graceful, mimicking the movement of the long-horned cattle. Women sway from side to side, while moving their hands in the air gracefully above their heads. This form of dancing is more relaxing, but the dancing by the

men from the western region is very energetic, with much jumping in the air and stamping of the feet, in *Riverdance* style.

Painting and Sculpture

In terms of fine art, there are a number of very talented artists, the best known being Taiga and Paulo Akiki. These artists usually sell their works

in dollars, but African art is still very cheap compared to art in Western countries. There are a number of good craft markets in Kampala (beside the National Theatre and along the Buganda Road) where one can buy crafts from the region, including African masks. Uganda does not have a local tradition of producing African masks, and the masks that are for sale are from the Congo. Other carvings originate from Uganda, Kenya, and Tanzania; baskets and mats are from Uganda, and Kisi stone carvings are from Kenya, though they are often finished in Uganda.

SOME MUST-SEE TOURIST ATTRACTIONS

- Mountain gorillas
- White-water rafting on the Nile
- Queen Elizabeth National Park
- Tree lions in Ishasha
- Chimps in Kibale Forest

- Kidepo National Park and the Karamajong
- The source of the Nile
- Murchison Falls
- Sipi Falls
- The Kabaka's Tombs
- Kabale and Lake Bunyonyi
- The crater lakes of Fort Portal

chapter seven

TRAVEL, HEALTH, & SAFETY

Uganda's network of roads is improving daily, so the journey to some of the far-flung game parks is no longer as arduous as it once was, though it still takes at least five hours to reach most game reserves from Kampala.

The road system in Kampala leaves much to be desired; the roads are narrow and driving competence could be said to vary from bad to dangerous, so it pays to take special care, even when one is a pedestrian. Sadly, the accident rate in Uganda, as in many African countries, is very high, and the visitor is statistically more likely to die in a road accident than through contracting HIV or an infectious disease. There are certain safety precautions that can be taken, such as not traveling at night, always wearing a helmet while on a motorcycle taxi, warning the driver (and even getting out of a taxi) if he appears to be driving recklessly, and making no assumptions that a motorcycle taxi will obey any traffic laws, such as going round a traffic circle in the right direction.

ARRIVAL

Currently people traveling to Uganda as tourists from outside the East African Community do

not need to buy visas in advance; the visa (US $50) can be paid for on arrival, either at the land border or at the airport. At the time of writing this book, an East African visa, allowing entrance into Kenya, Uganda, and Rwanda, is about to be introduced. This visa will allow multiple entries for three months, at a cost of US $100. It can be purchased at the border on entry, or at the embassies of the participating countries.

Entebbe Airport has been refurbished recently and is one of the more pleasant airports in the region. The immigration staff are generally friendly, efficient, and helpful, and one will sometimes be greeted by a smile and a "Welcome to Uganda." The airport is just under twenty-five miles (40 k) from Kampala, and the journey will take one to two hours, depending on the traffic. There are many airport taxis and transfers. The taxi ride to Kampala will cost at least 80–90,000 Uganda shillings (US $35).

GETTING AROUND TOWN

The most common mode of transportation is
the *matatu*, or fourteen-seat minibus taxi, which
plies the roads all over Uganda; added to this are
the ubiquitous *boda bodas*, the small 100cc Indian
Boxer motorcycle taxis. There are about sixty
thousand of these in the Kampala area alone,
swarming around like mosquitoes. The name
boda boda comes from Border–Border: when

there was a no-man's-land between the Kenyan and Ugandan borders in the 1960s bicycles were used to ferry people between them. Bicycles are still used but have been overtaken by motorcycles over the past decade.

The motorcycles are very convenient, but since the roads are so congested, and some of the young men who ride them have more bravado than road sense, there are many accidents resulting in serious injuries, because, apart from a few *bazungu* (foreigners), it is rare to find passengers wearing helmets. *Boda bodas* also carry a diverse range of cargo and a variable number of passengers, which can range from as many as four adults (in which case the driver is perched on the fuel tank), to a suite of furniture, fifty chickens, or twenty trays of eggs (not hard boiled).

Potholes

Owing to the poor quality of the roads in Kampala, and the lack of maintenance over a prolonged period of time, some of the roads have

broken down into potholes. Since the roads are already crowded, the sudden appearance of even one big pothole at a junction can slow the traffic further. Much time was being lost as motorists sat in traffic jams, so under the new administration in Kampala (Kampala Capital City Authority) fixing potholes has become a priority, and the number of potholes has decreased noticeably, with the flow of traffic consequently improving—except when it rains. However, potholes have a habit of rearranging themselves, and no sooner has one been fixed than another pops open a few meters away, so the battle continues.

Rain

For some reason, when it rains in Uganda life comes to a standstill. This is inexplicable: it can't be that the rain catches people off guard, or that they are not prepared for it, as it rains regularly and often. But inevitably if it rains there are traffic jams, people are late for work, and no one even feels the need to give an explanation, since everyone knows it has rained. This is apparently a good enough reason for being late, missing meetings and deadlines, or any sort of problem that one may have in life.

The best way to get through the traffic in Kampala is during the rain itself, as there will be little traffic on the roads. It seems that people cannot make it from their homes to their cars or the taxi in the rain, so no one sets out on the journey. Unfortunately after the rain everyone then sets out together, and there is total gridlock, made worse by the inevitable flooding of the low-lying areas. The reason for all this is because of Ugandan women's hair, which cannot on any account be taken out in the rain. Apparently the rain is the worst thing that can happen to African hair, and the last thing any sane Ugandan woman will do is go out in it.

DRIVING

Driving in Uganda is not for the fainthearted. Vehicles drive on the left, as in Britain, and the rules are basically the same as in the British Highway Code, but few drivers are familiar with this document. Bad driving is endemic, because people don't learn to drive properly in the first place. Although there is a proper system for applying for a provisional license, having instruction, and passing a test, it is common practice to buy a car and then simply get in and start driving. So drivers cut corners and drift from lane to lane, since they have never learned that they should turn a T-junction at a right angle, and have no idea what a lane is.

Driving with Sang-Froid

I have a friend who bought a small car (small cars are known as "my cars" in Uganda, because the new owner says "I now have my car"), even though she did not know how to drive. Spontaneous dents, which she could not explain, then began to appear on the bodywork. Eventually she took her test, and might even have passed but for her inability to manage parallel parking, so she failed. Needless to say, she carried on driving.

The other menace to drivers of four-wheeled vehicles are the *boda bodas*, since they are ridden by young boys whose only qualification is a high level of fatalism. *Boda bodas* get people to their destination rapidly—except for those who die in the process. The Ugandan Police recently decreed that *boda boda* riders should wear helmets (a reasonable health and safety feature today), but for some reason, possibly to do with female African hairstyles that do not fit into the helmets, passengers were exempted. So the passengers seldom wear helmets, while the drivers wear helmets without a strap, or ones that are too big, or else they place the helmet on the handlebars.

Should a motorist have the misfortune to collide with a *boda boda,* there is an unwritten rule that it is always the fault of the motorist, who will take the rider to hospital, pay the bill, and also pay to have the motorcycle repaired.

INTERCITY TRANSPORT

Between the towns, public transport is available in the form of large buses. It is wise to be vigilant when using these, since foreigners can be targeted by conmen. Some innocent visitors have accepted a cookie (from a sealed packet) from the friendly person sitting beside them, only to wake up at the end of the journey with none of their personal belongings—they have been drugged. So, as your mother always told you, don't accept food from strangers.

Along the route there are various stops, where roadside vendors will pass food such as meat on skewers, *gonja* (fried bananas), fried cassava, and soft drinks through the windows to the passengers. The food is cheap, though it is best to stick to the vegetarian options.

On public transport personal space may be limited, since one may be sharing not only with the other passengers packed in like sardines, but with their livestock, particularly chickens. Buses have seating limits, above which they are not supposed to overload, but the drivers tend to push in more passengers because they make more money. In the smaller *matatus* there is an upper limit of fourteen people, which the police enforce on the main roads, but on the minor roads the number of people is determined by how many can be physically squeezed in.

WHERE TO STAY

There are various types of accommodation to be had, varying from cheap lodges and backpackers' hostels to guesthouses and hotels. The business community will normally opt for the recognized names, such as the Sheraton, the Serena, or the Proteus, while backpackers will gravitate to one of the hostels, of which there are two in Kampala and several in Jinja. There are many small, cheap hotels scattered throughout Uganda, most of which are quite adequate, and all of which provide a pair of flip-flops for the bathroom, which is normally of an acceptable Western standard. The backpackers' hostels are relatively cheap, but one will only meet other backpackers and few locals there unless you venture outside to the local pub or church.

Staying in a Ugandan Home

It is not common for visitors to stay in Ugandans' homes, unless they are staying with friends, probably because few organizations have a system for this. One organization that runs a successful cultural exchange with home-stays is the School for International Training, a USA-based non-profit educational institute.

If you are staying in a local home, however, it is wise to come with a mosquito net, since no matter how good the accommodation there are likely to be mosquitoes. Otherwise the experience is well worthwhile, and usually results in lifelong friendships.

HEALTH

Visitors to Uganda must have a yellow fever vaccination several weeks before departure. While Uganda does not strictly enforce this rule, other surrounding countries do, and it is sensible to have the vaccination before setting out. Other inoculations are fairly standard: tetanus, Hepatitis A and B (particularly if one is going to work in a medical context), meningitis, and typhoid. It is also necessary to commence anti-malarial prophylaxis a week before setting out.

Health insurance for travelers is relatively cheap, and it is essential not to leave home without it. Standards at local health centers vary, and they will generally diagnose malaria as a matter of course, even if it is not present. If you have a fever, it is vital to go to a reputable facility for an accurate diagnosis. Even the expensive health facilities are relatively cheap compared to hospitals in Europe or America.

Health Hazards
Malaria
The word for malaria in Uganda is *musuja*, which is also the word for fever, so there is a paradox that when a patient goes to see the doctor with

musuja, he is informing the doctor of the diagnosis. The result is that practically every ailment that falls into the category of fever is treated as malaria. This, of course, has resulted in the over-diagnosis and over-treatment of malaria, resulting in the development of resistance to drugs such as chloroquine. Most tourists take anti-malarial prophylaxis, which is the wise course of action, but there are some who think they can get away with not taking the tablets, and this is risky. The correct advice for short-term travelers is to take prophylaxis—either malarone, doxycyline, or mefloquine—and also sleep under a treated mosquito net. In a few individuals there may be some side effects from these drugs—such as vivid dreams, mood swings, or nausea—which are usually cited as the reasons for opting out. If you develop any minor flulike symptoms when you return home, is important that you inform the doctor you have been traveling in a malarial area.

Malaria is more common in certain parts of Uganda, and during certain seasons, mainly when it is hot and wet. If you stay in an upscale area of Kampala you are unlikely to get malaria, but if you travel to the game parks your chances of being infected are higher. A person on prophylaxis is unlikely to develop malaria, and those who are at risk are the workers and residents who decide not to take prophylaxis because they are living in the country for a longer period. Such people should use treated mosquito nets and go for a test if they develop any fever. Sadly there are regular deaths among expatriates from malaria, most of which are avoidable.

HIV
Although the prevalence of HIV is high at almost
7 percent, a person will not catch it from casual
contact. The transmission of HIV in Uganda is
mainly through heterosexual sex, and the best
advice for the traveler is to abstain from sex with
anyone whose HIV status is unknown. It is very easy
to go along to a clinic with your partner for an HIV
test, but there is also a window period of about six
weeks during which a recently infected person
would not show as positive, so condoms are advised.
Sex with a properly used condom is safe. Given that
alcohol is relatively cheap and plentiful, it is not
uncommon for someone who is drinking to have
impaired judgment and end up in a compromising
situation. If you feel there is any possibility that this
could happen, it is best to be armed with a condom,
but should the deed be done without a condom,
both partners should go along to a reputable clinic
for a test the next day. Should your partner be found
to be positive, it is best to take post-exposure
prophylaxis, starting immediately.

Ebola
Ebola and other infectious hemorrhagic fevers have
had much publicity in Uganda and Congo, but the
chances of an ordinary tourist coming into contact
with them is slim to none.

Bilharzia
If contemplating swimming in the lakes, one should
know that schistosomes, which transmit bilharzia,
are endemic in many lakes. This little flatworm is
spread through urination in the water from infected
communities living on the shores of the lake. It

passes through a snail as an intermediate host and in its next stage can penetrate the legs of swimmers and move into the blood vessels of the bladder or the gastrointestinal tract. Some of the worms may end up in the spinal cord or the brain, which can cause seizures or paralysis. Although such cases are very rare, the possibility gives people pause before jumping into Lake Victoria. One should note that fast-flowing waters are not as susceptible to bilharzia, and white-water rafters are therefore much less likely to get infected. Some swimmers and boaters on the lake take regular doses of the anti-bilharzia medicine Praziquantel.

SAFETY AND THEFT

Compared to other African countries, such as South Africa or Kenya, Uganda is fairly safe, but this is relative, and depends on where you are, what time it is, and who you are with. If you are careless or too trusting, you are asking for trouble. Unfortunately it has now become common practice at the scene of a car accident for the victims to be robbed.

It is unwise for a girl to be out alone at night, and she should not get into a taxi or on to a *boda boda* without knowing the driver. Girls should always travel together, preferably in the company of male friends. Although Uganda is relatively safe, there are still instances where foreign girls have been raped, and theft is relatively common, but making sensible plans and taking precautions can ensure against such dangers. It is usually possible to get to know a taxi driver who is linked to the hotel or the place where you are staying, and use him for drop-offs and pick-ups at night.

DEALING WITH THE POLICE

As a rule the traffic police are polite, though some may try to instill fear on first meeting in order to soften you up for any negotiation that may take place. Traffic police are easily recognized by the white uniforms they wear. The fines for traffic offenses are now quite high—200,000 Uganda shillings (US $75) for speeding, for example. If you have committed a traffic offense you may be fined, in which case you will be issued with a ticket showing the amount of money you have to pay at the bank (you don't pay the police directly) and you will be asked for your license. Or you may just be warned and allowed to proceed. In this case the policeman may also inform you that it is a hot day, and whether you give him the price of a soda is up to you, though this is technically a bribe. Instead of giving you the official fine, some will use the opportunity to negotiate a lower "on the spot fine," which will go to the policeman's beneficiary fund. Should this be the case, the police officer has a name and a number and can be reported at the nearest police station, since the head of the police takes a very dim view of bribery.

There are other police who travel in patrols or answer emergency calls. They wear khaki or black uniforms, are usually heavily armed, and can be very intimidating—but if they are not wearing white they are not traffic police. It may be that they have seen you doing something wrong, such as talking on your cell phone while driving, which is illegal. If you are stopped by a mobile patrol, officially they have to take you to the traffic police, but in the face of six or eight heavily armed policemen one may be inclined to cooperate.

chapter eight

BUSINESS BRIEFING

THE BUSINESS CLIMATE

There are many business opportunities for foreign investors, and the major issue is finding one's way through the system. There are other challenges, such as poor infrastructure in the form of roads, railways, and electricity, but the government is working to remedy these bottlenecks.

Most Ugandans will tell you that doing business in Uganda is easy, but this is because they will automatically know their way around the system and "know people who know people." For this reason some foreign investors feel that they need a local partner. In fact, this depends on both the proposed partner and the area of business being

embarked upon. A good local partner can be very helpful, but so is a good lawyer, and the Ugandan business system is designed to attract foreign investment directly, without the legal necessity of having a local partner.

Like other countries, Uganda is rated on a World Bank Report "ease of doing business" index. To give a comparison in the ratings of 1–185, with 1 being the country that is most business friendly, the number one spot goes to Singapore. The USA is fourth. The most difficult country in which to do business is the Central African Republic, at 185. Uganda ranks 120, with Kenya at 121, Tanzania at 132, and Congo at 183, while the star of the region is Rwanda, at 52.

The first place for a potential investor to visit is the Uganda Investment Authority, which is intended to be a one-stop shop for the various business and tax registrations. It is not exactly one-stop, but will definitely help as a guide to the various agencies one has to deal with.

There are different sectors with potential for development within Uganda, the most recent being the oil sector. This has attracted some of the big players, including Total, the Chinese National Offshore Oil Corporation (CNOOC), and Tullow Oil. The oil sector is now preparing for the extractive phase, which will create many jobs and opportunities for supporting services within Uganda.

Foreigners cannot buy land in Uganda, but can lease land on a renewable lease for up to ninety-nine years. This leasehold is effectively the same as purchasing the land, and is not a hindrance to doing business. However, the system for identifying a suitable piece of land can be fraught, and despite the recent computerization of the land office and land register, there are many people who have been duped by land scams. There are a number of highly professional and reputable law firms that can look after one's interests, and although these firms may appear to be expensive, they are well worth the investment in guiding one though the process of doing business in Uganda.

LAND SCAMS

Many ordinary Ugandans have been caught in land scams, in which they think they are buying a piece of land with a bona fide title, and then find that the same plot has been sold several times over and their title is a fake. One lady arrived to check out her newly purchased piece of land, to find several others, all of whom had been sold the same plot, doing the same thing. Ugandans call this "buying air."

Land can be registered under several different types of registration. There is Milo Land, Kabaka Land, private freehold land, and leasehold land. There are also several land boards, including a Kampala Land Board, District Land Boards, and the Land Registry Office. There are also different bodies that give permission to develop land, such as the Kampala Capital City Authority, and the various district administrations, plus the National Environmental Authority (NEMA), which designates wetlands.

DEALING WITH THE GOVERNMENT

Many potential investors beat a pathway to the door of the president. There are those who claim they work in State House and can fix an appointment for a fee, but it is not necessary to see the president unless there is some area that needs his intervention, and many times this introduces unnecessary politicization. Visiting high-level government bureaucrats can also be frustrating, since if they have some higher priority they will break the appointment or keep you waiting for a long time. One just has to be patient, stay polite, and keep smiling.

PREMISES

There is a surplus of newly built office space in Kampala, which has not yet translated into cheaper rents but gives a greater choice of locations. There are also a number of businesses and NGOs that have rented residential houses in secondary locations; these are much cheaper than Central Business District office property, and the planning laws for mixed residential use allow residential and office use in the same area.

BUSINESS CULTURE

Businessmen working in Uganda include Ugandans, Ugandan Asians, Kenyans, South Sudanese, Somalis, and expatriate businessmen from all countries, with an increasingly large Chinese presence. There is a strong corporate culture, with regular business launches and marketing events where one can meet people. Uganda may be a country of thirty-four million people, but the Kampala business community is relatively small, and it is certainly a good policy to keep on good terms with everybody, since one will meet the same people again in different circumstances.

The management structure of companies varies according to their size, with large companies having the normal corporate governance structure, while small to medium-sized companies may be owned and run by individuals and families. There are some very large Ugandan Asian businesses in manufacturing, transport, property, tea, and sugar estates, and there are a number of very successful Ugandan African businessmen who have interests in telecoms, oil, hotels, and farming. Banks, insurance companies, and companies working in the financial sector are highly regulated, and the oil and mining sector is developing strong regulation.

In terms of administrative, unskilled, and semi-skilled labor, there is no shortage, though there are gaps in sectors that require specialized or highly skilled work. There are various trade unions, which are not usually highly adversarial in their approach to negotiations.

DRESS CODE

In the formal business sector and the public sector the dress code is relatively formal, with most people wearing dark business suits and ties, so although one may not wish to walk around in a

suit all day, it is useful to keep a jacket in the car, or a spare jacket at the office—one wouldn't want to stand out at a business briefing, or the after-work business cocktail, as the only person not wearing a dark jacket. Because it is a relatively small community, it is possible to get to know the CEOs of all the banks, the heads of the large parastatals (companies or agencies owned or controlled wholly or partly by the government), permanent secretaries, and the wealthy entrepreneurs who know all the deals. It is also possible to attend useful budget and business briefings of organizations such as PWC and IMF, and marketing functions from companies launching new products, particularly in the telecoms and drinks industries.

SETTING UP A BUSINESS MEETING

There is no set formula for arranging a meeting. Some people simply arrive in the country and start making phone calls, but it will be easier if you have made prior contact by e-mail. If you have engaged a local law firm as a local representative, you can ask it to set up the meeting. Important people will be busy, and many businessmen travel frequently in the region. An e-mail is the best way to initiate contact, followed by a phone call to confirm the appointment. For government ministries there is a constant process of calling to confirm, since the minister may travel on short notice, or have an urgent cabinet meeting to attend. It is always good practice to get the name and, if possible, the cell phone number of the personal assistant, as well as the cell number of the person you wish to meet—the PA will be helpful in setting up the appointment as he or she is the keeper of the diary.

MEETINGS

It is important to be on time for a business meeting, even in the government sector where the official may keep you waiting; turning up late makes a bad first impression. Dress code among Ugandan officials is normally a suit, but a shirt and jacket worn without a tie is perfectly acceptable, and if it is a warm day no one will object to your removing the jacket. The presentation of business cards is important; even though it is not a formal exchange, as in the Far East, it does serve to give everyone something to focus on—and play with.

If the meeting is in a boardroom, people tend to assemble in "teams" on either side of the table, with the seat at the head left for the minister or the CEO. You can break the ice with small talk, especially if you have gained some local knowledge, but this is cursory, and you can get down to business quickly.

A simple, clear, authoritative presentation, either on PowerPoint or verbally, will be a good starting point for discussion. The presentation should not be long or complicated, and you should be prepared to take questions either during or after the presentation. There are likely to be interruptions to most meetings, except at very high levels.

NEGOTIATIONS

If you are having a preliminary meeting to explore a business relationship or deal, it is not necessary to have lawyers present, but when getting into details it is important to have a lawyer with you for guidance, though don't make the mistake of allowing the lawyer to take over the negotiations.

Negotiations are generally good humored, and Ugandans will appreciate a friendly approach rather than formality and stiffness. The rule of thumb is that if you smile or make a joke they will join you in the joke, and if you are serious and formal they will take their cue from you. Ugandan Asians are tough negotiators and will play hardball. Government officials may have a hidden agenda, and you must ensure that you are both on the same page and that you understand what they want.

All Ugandan businessmen who run small to medium-sized businesses tend to see the value of their business in terms of assets—more so than in EBITA or net profit—and may not have the means to prove that their company is as profitable as they claim. Of course one will expect to see properly audited accounts for larger businesses. Serious negotiations will be held with the principals of the business, and if you are handed over to a junior the business owner is probably not taking you seriously. It is always best to verify ownership and then go to the top

CONTRACTS AND FULFILLMENT

Contracts are binding once they are signed and registered, and the deal is not sealed until all the details have been sorted out. The handshake denotes intent, but the difference is in the detail— which is in the contract.

If a contract is breached, the settlement can be informal, otherwise it will go to a process of arbitration at the commercial court, and if it cannot be settled through this it will go formally to the commercial court for judgment. If you find yourself in a dispute over breach of contract some Ugandan businessmen will assume that they have the upper hand, since the court process can take time and they hope that the foreigner will give up. The courts are generally reliable.

In terms of employment law and work practices, the processes are clearly set down and one is expected to stick to them. Some foreign companies have been called out for firing an employee, for example, for theft, but failing to follow the process of reporting the case to the police and awaiting the outcome. Then the staff member takes the company to court for unfair dismissal. In a case where it is strongly suspected that someone is stealing but there is a lack of definite proof, it is best to let the person go under the normal terms of the contract.

WOMEN IN BUSINESS

There is no resistance to doing business with women in high places. Women in Uganda occupy many influential positions, including Speaker of Parliament, Director General of the Uganda Revenue Authority, Minister of Finance, Executive Director of Kampala Capital City Authority, CEOs of several banks, and many senior management positions in business. While there are a few foreign businesswomen in the country, foreign women more usually occupy high positions in aid agencies and the diplomatic community as ambassadors and heads of missions.

GIFT GIVING

It is always good to acknowledge a good relationship or good service with a "thank you," but this should be appropriate—a bottle of wine or whiskey, or a gift basket, are all very acceptable. It is also appropriate to bring something "national" from your own country, or an engraved gift denoting the significant event, accompanied by a photo opportunity.

CORRUPTION

Over the years, corruption has become a big issue throughout Uganda, because it is not limited simply to one group of people. It is not just politicians, or those working in the public sector, who are corrupt; corruption is pervasive throughout society. This is not to create the impression that Ugandan society is so corrupt that it is dysfunctional, like some neighboring countries in central Africa. Society functions relatively well, and many people do their jobs very well. However, there is a sense across a large swathe of society that if there is an  opportunity for enrichment, it should be exploited. This can vary from behavior such as stealing the fuel of the official vehicle to expecting commissions on contracts, or procurement officers negotiating a higher price for their company rather than a lower one, in order to be paid the difference.

One must ascertain the bona fides of the person or company with whom one is dealing, and therefore whether there will be a reasonable chance that the deal can be done honestly. There is no point in investing time and effort into bidding for contracts that are already fixed. However, there are many honest companies and government officials operating in Uganda with whom one can still do business. In today's environment in Uganda, where the public sector is under scrutiny regarding corruption, it is unlikely that a high-level minister or official will come straight out and ask for a bribe, but in some cases hints may be dropped, which can then be ignored without causing offense.

chapter nine

COMMUNICATING

LANGUAGE

The official language in Uganda is English, but Luganda is *de facto* the national language in that it is widely spoken, much more than Swahili, the language of trade in East Africa. Swahili is a costal trading language that is widely used in Tanzania, less so in Kenya, and hardly at all in Uganda. In Uganda it came to be associated with the brutalities of the army under the regimes of Milton Obote and Idi Amin, and hence is avoided by ordinary people.

Almost all Ugandans also speak their own tribal language, even if they have not grown up in the tribal area. Thus educated Ugandans are fluent in English and their tribal language. They may also speak a smattering of Swahili, and since much of the formal education takes place in central Uganda, that is, Buganda, most Ugandans also speak some Luganda. Even if English is the formal medium of teaching, students pick Luganda up at school (since they will not get the jokes if they don't understand it). Of course the Baganda themselves are fluent in Luganda, as it is spoken in the home; a Muganda who is poorly educated will speak primarily Luganda, with a smattering of English, but a Muganda who has been educated to a second-grade level will be bilingual, though he may mix Luganda and English when he is speaking, which has become known as Luganglish. It relatively easy to get the drift of what someone is saying by picking up the key English phrases. On the other hand, northerners are proud of their own language and traditions, and are much less willing to speak Luganda. As a result they often speak good English, though with a pronounced northern accent.

Ugandan English

Some of the expressions used in Ugandan English are direct translations from the vernacular, while some Ugandans use English in a way that makes sense only when you realize they have used a noun as a verb, or slightly changed the accepted meaning of a word or phrase. For example, if you ask directions, you might be told to "slope down" to the bottom of the hill, then "extend a bit" along the road, until you reach the big tree. In English, when the subject is a person we might use the verb "slope" in a sentence such as "the man sloped off ashamedly," or when describing a hill we can say it slopes, but how does a person slope down? In Uganda it makes perfect sense—instead of going down the slope, you simply slope down: the hill doesn't slope, you slope down it.

Slope Inn
Apropos "sloping down" the hill, there is a guesthouse located on the slope of a hill on the outskirts of Kampala actually named "Slope Inn." I don't know whether the name is an invitation to slope into the guesthouse for some illicit activity, or if it's named after the slope of the hill.

The command "extend" is used surprisingly often, but while we generally understand the verb "to extend" in the context of extending an arm, or extending the size of something, in Uganda it is commonly used to mean simply move over or move along. A driver in a *matatu* (minibus taxi) may tell you to "extend a bit," or someone may mean it in the sense of moving further along the road, so when you are told "you extend a bit," it does not mean that you should puff up and get bigger, just move a bit.

In the Ugandan English the letters "r" and "l" can be interchanged, and the "r" is commonly not pronounced, which can be very confusing. The cleric in church may announce, "Let us play. Lord, we thank you for the blead and the wine." Mixing up "l" and "r" is worse during elections, or "erections." When someone does not understand the concept of a silent "ed" they pronounce rigged as "rigid." So if they tell you that the election was rigged, it can come out as "the erection was rigid." Other peculiarities include "Happy Bathday" for "Happy Birthday," and "bird" is "bad," since the "r" is not pronounced. This can also lead to confusion, as when Bird Flu was a threat and the Mayor of Kampala assured people "'Good Flu, Bad Flu,' we will handle it."

English words and expressions don't always have the same meanings in Uganda as in the recognized English dictionaries, so if someone describes another person, particularly a child, as "stubborn," they don't necessarily mean that the child is not easily persuaded, but that he is rebellious. In fact this word has a whole range of meanings that don't necessarily have an equivalent in the English language, so if someone tells you that you are stubborn, don't get too upset—they might just mean that you are different.

Also, if someone is referred to as having "bad manners," it does not mean that his table manners are bad; it has the sense that he was badly brought up, which is quite an insult. If you tell someone he is "not serious," it is also an insult. While we use the expression "You're not serious!" as an exclamation, in Uganda it means that the person is not serious about his work, or even about life, and is not a person who can be relied upon.

EXPRESSIONS REGARDING TIME

It is important to understand what a person means when you call him up and ask where he is.

- If he says he is "about" to come, that might mean that he is around the corner, or that he is has not left home yet but is about to leave. But if he says, "Let me come," that means he has definitely not set out yet. "Let me come" is the literal translation of the Luganda word "Kanseja", which has the connotation of coming if there are no hindrances; it is an expression of vague intent, not of urgent prioritization.

- If you go to an office and are told that someone has "just stepped out," it means that his colleagues are covering for him and have no idea where he is. His coat may be on the back of his chair, but you should probably not wait around as this is no guarantee that he will be back shortly; he could be in the next town doing a business deal.

FORMS OF ADDRESS

The many public gatherings in Uganda—weddings, funerals, political meetings, or meetings called by government and NGOs to launch some initiative—follow a certain protocol, which is observed both in the order of the speakers and in the titles given to them. The meeting is welcomed by the chairman of the village council, followed by the chairman of the parish. Then the speakers are called in order of seniority, until one reaches the guest of honor, who gives the main speech.

Most speakers start by listing the titles of the important people who are there. All members of parliament, including past members, are prefixed by the term "Honorable." The practice is to refer to all members of parliament at all times as "Honorable" in the same way as one gives the title of "Doctor" to a medic. This does not follow the procedure of the "Mother of Parliaments," where the term is reserved for addressing the member on the floor of the House; but titles are important in Africa and are used lavishly.

One commonly used method of addressing people, which makes it easy if one has difficulty remembering names, is to use the title of the person's profession. Thus someone who has trained as an engineer can simply be addressed as "Engineer"; similarly all medical people tend to be addressed as "Doctor," whether a veterinary doctor, a dentist, or even those who have lower levels of qualifications such as nurses or clinical officers (the local term for doctor is *Musawo*). This habit of calling people Doctor/*Musawo* often extends to people with absolutely no qualifications, but who may have worked in a hospital or run a shop selling

medicines, so they become known as "doctors."
People are also referred to by titles such as
"Chairman" if they hold local office, or "Hajj" if
they have completed the Muslim pilgrimage, or
"Hajjet" in the case of the wife.

GREETINGS AND GOOD MANNERS

Ugandans are naturally polite and well mannered.
A Ugandan will not wish to walk between two
people having a conversation in a corridor, and
if there is not enough room to walk around them,
he may hover until they move, so that he can
pass behind them.

Ugandan children are taught to greet adults
politely and shake hands; they will also go down
on their knees when they greet elders. When
asking directions, foreigners have a habit of
simply going up to a person and asking the
question. Ugandans will not do this; first they
will greet the person, preferably thanking him for
whatever he is doing at the time, or just thanking
him for nothing in particular. At that point the
inquirer can then go on to ask for directions, and
if one is in a vehicle it would not be unusual for
the stranger to get into the car to show you the
way. If a foreigner forgets to greet and launches
straight into the question, the Ugandan will pause,
then greet him before answering.

Handshakes

There are different ways of greeting people, and
a mixture of Western and traditional forms of
greeting have been adopted. The reserved, polite
way to greet an elder or superior is the handshake

with a slight bow. If one is greeting an elder with a hug this is acceptable, but one stands slightly away from the person, bends toward them and hugs one shoulder and then the other, with a small pat on the back. This is a sign of affection, without being too up close and personal.

Most Ugandan girls like to hug their peers in the normal Western style, while men will give a firm handshake, or a handshake with the shoulder bump if you are good friends.

The East African Handshake

Ugandans sometimes shake hands using the normal handshake followed by a thumb grip, then sliding back to a normal handshake and repeating the movement. The trick is to know when to let go, because if you stop too soon the other person will be left grabbing air, and if you keep holding on the process could last indefinitely.

Someone may shake your hand and then continue holding it because he wants to talk to you. It is quite normal for men to hold hands with men, and for men and women to hold hands without any particular significance except friendship.

Sitting Down

Unlike in Western societies, where someone coming into the room may wait until they are invited to sit down, Ugandans will come into the room and automatically take a seat. This is because it is rude for them to stand while you are seated. Normally in a village home, the men will sit on chairs or stools, while the women will sit on mats on the floor.

When someone is signaling for you to come over, he will stretch out his hand, palm down, and move his fingers toward his palm, the opposite of the palm-up style of beckoning.

When men and women are working in the fields, or doing work in which they have to bend over, they bend at the hip; they will never squat, since squatting is associated with relieving oneself and the posture is rude.

BODY LANGUAGE

Some Ugandans have the ability to answer a question without the actual use of language and with minimal movement of the facial muscles. For example, if you ask for directions the person may incline her head in the general direction and then point with her lips—an effective way of communicating and conserving movement.

The other gesture that keeps movement to the minimum is to say "yes" with the eyebrows. This takes some getting used to. If you ask a question that requires a "yes" or "no" answer, and they move their eyebrows it means "yes," or at least is an acknowledgment that they have understood ("no" in this case would be denoted by no movement whatsoever). Both of these movements can be open to misinterpretation in the same way that Indians tilting their heads from side to side to mean "yes" may confuse a foreigner, but once you get the hang of the lips and the eyebrows they are quite clear.

THE MEDIA
The Press

Uganda has a number of newspapers, with the highest circulation going to the *New Vision*, which has a significant government shareholding and is sometimes seen as a government mouthpiece. The *Daily Monitor* is perceived as an opposition newspaper, but has no connection with the Ugandan political opposition and is owned by the Aga Khan Foundation, a liberal philanthropic organization with Islamic roots. Other newspapers and magazines include the *Observer*, the *Red Pepper* (a tabloid akin to the *Racing Press* or *National Inquirer*) and the *Independent*.

Uganda has had poor international press coverage because of the bill passed through parliament making the soliciting of gay sex a crime punishable by life imprisonment. The bill is poorly framed, and draconian in its penalties. Uganda has also had a bad press due to the temporary closure of several media houses in 2013 as part of an investigation into allegations by an army general that there was a plot to overthrow the government. The way in which the government handled the affair gave the allegations more credibility than they deserved, and was an international public relations disaster.

The paradox is that government is generally tolerant of the media, and of individual freedoms, to the point where it is possible for people to go on radio stations and make all manner of false comments and unfounded allegations, or for a newspaper to print stories with very little factual basis. However, from time to time some comment or newspaper article sparks an overreaction by the government and the police, resulting in a clampdown. As a generalization, one can say there is free speech in Uganda, though the closing down of media organizations could be a warning that this freedom should not be taken for granted. In 2013 the government also passed the Public Order Bill. This gave the police wide powers over the authorization of public gatherings, which was seen as a means of hamstringing the opposition, making it difficult for them to organize political rallies.

Television and Radio

There are six local TV stations and more than a hundred local radio stations, but most broadcast within a limited radius. The local news content, particularly on NTV Uganda, is very good, and news bulletins are broadcast in Luganda and English. There are a number of locally produced soap operas, regional talent competitions, and the ubiquitous Big Brother Africa, drawing hopefuls from across the continent.

Most Ugandans get to know what is going on through listening to their local radio stations in the vernacular; every district and town has a radio station that broadcasts news and opinion. There are also national stations that target certain audiences such as young people, middle-aged upper-income groups, and so on. The debates on politics are lively, though sometimes the fact checking leaves something to be desired.

SERVICES
Telephone

There are a number of cell phone operators in Uganda, and the ownership of phones within the population has risen massively over the past decade. It is now the norm for most adults to have phones, and even aged relatives in remote villages can be contacted. MTN is the largest operator, with Airtel (Baharti Telecom) having gained ground. Orange is well established, particularly for Internet services, and 3G services, which are much faster, have now been introduced by several companies including Smile, MTN, and Orange. The official telecom company, Uganda Telecom, appears to have fallen behind in the race.

Internet

Internet connectivity is slow and expensive compared to that in Europe or America, but the speeds are improving and, as in all parts of the world, the Internet has changed the way people communicate and do business. With the availability of dongles (Wi-Fi adapters) there is nowhere one

cannot find a connection. Ugandans are active on
social media, and there are lively debates on all
issues, such as the Anti-Homosexuality Bill, the
Anti-Pornography Bill, and the Public Order Bill,
on Facebook and Twitter.

Mail

The Ugandan Post Office service is sometimes
erratic, and if one has a document or parcel that
must be transported reliably, it is best to use one
of the courier services, of which there are several,
the best known being DHL.

CONCLUSION

When one is thinking of a trip to Africa, or of
doing business in Africa, Uganda may not spring
to mind as the first option in the way that South
Africa or Kenya present themselves. Such countries
are relatively well developed and also offer the
expected benefits of going on safari to see big
game. Recently Uganda has not done itself any
favors in how it is perceived, because of the passing
of the anti-gay legislation. However, superficial
perceptions are not where the truth lies: Uganda
offers all the usual tourist attractions and more,
including mountain gorillas and white-water
rafting, and, far from being intolerant, the
Ugandan character is broadly tolerant and open.

Perhaps it is "international pressure" that
sometimes makes Ugandans react in a manner that
says, "I have my own culture and values and I don't
need you [the international community] to lecture
me." A thorough understanding of another nation's
culture is not easy, since in today's world most

nations have a veneer of modernity that makes them appear Westernized, but respecting the cultural values of another people should not be difficult. Ugandans accept modern Western cultural values, but beneath this they also have traditional values—of family, tribe, and culture—that they expect Westerners to respect in return.

They have a sixth sense, like radar, which tells them when they are being judged and when they are being accepted. Many modern Western nations are very sure of their own value systems and cannot imagine a different paradigm. However, there are other norms and yardsticks that are part of the fabric of Ugandan society. One may not agree with them, but neither should one stand in judgment, apart from on issues of basic human rights.

Basically, if one accepts Ugandans they will accept you. This does not require you to create a rosy, unrealistic picture of the country, but it means acceptance, warts and all. One can recognize the corruption, the politics, the crying need for training and youth employment, the very real social issues. But one should also appreciate the irrepressible joy of Ugandan society, the love of life, the laughter, the sheer ability to make the best of the conditions, the interest in you as a stranger, the acceptance of who you are and who they are.

Uganda is a country that has many problems to deal with, in terms of development and ending the cycle of poverty for many of its citizens, but it not only has amazing natural beauty—which is often hidden unless you go looking—it has real beauty in its people. As with the beauty of the country, you may have to dig a little more deeply to appreciate the beauty of Ugandans themselves.

Further Reading

Breitinger, Eckhard. *Uganda: The Cultural Landscape*. Kampala: Fountain Publishers, 2000.

Briggs, Philip, with Andrew Roberts. *Bradt Guide: Uganda (6th edition)*. Chalfont St. Peters, UK: Bradt Travel Guides, 2013.

Clarke, Dr. Ian. *The Man With the Key Has Gone!* Chichester: New Wine Press, 1993.

_____*How Deep is this Pothole?* Chichester: New Wine Press, 2010.

De Temmerman, Els. *The Aboke Girls*. Kampala: Fountain Publishers, 2001.

Hanson, Thor. *The Impenetrable Forest: My Gorilla Years in Uganda*. 1500 Books, Revised ed. 2008; New York: Curtis Brown Unlimited, 2014.

Kyemba, Henry. *A State of Blood: The Inside Story of Idi Amin*. Kampala: Fountain Publishers, 1997.

Mugyenyi, Peter. *Genocide by Denial: How Profiteering From HIV/AIDS Killed Millions*. Kampala: Fountain Publishers, 2008.

Nyamweru, Celia, and Catherine Gombe. *Barkcloth in Uganda: The Modern Day Importance of an Indigenous Craft*. Lambert Academic Publishing, 2012.

Rice, Andrew. *The Teeth May Smile but the Heart Does Not Forget*. New York: Metropolitan Books, 2009.

Rugazira, Andrew. *A Good African Story*. London: The Bodley Head, 2013.

Tumusiime, James (executive editor) *People and Cultures of Uganda (4th edition)*. Kampala: Fountain Publishers, 2011.

Fiction

Gee, Maggie. *My Cleaner*. London: Telegram Books, 2006.

_____*My Driver*. London: Telegram Books, 2009.

Foden, Giles. *The Last King of Scotland*. London: Faber and Faber, 1998.

Isegawa, Moses. *Abyssinian Chronicles*. London: Picador, 2001.

Kibuuka, Ulysses C. *Of Saints and Scarecrows*. Kampala: Fountain Publishers, 2007.

Index

Acknowledgments

I would like to acknowledge the invaluable input from my wife, Robbie.
I would also like to acknowledge all the Ugandans with whom I have
worked over the years at International Medical Group and Kiwoko
Hospital, who have given me a love for Uganda and Ugandans.